HELP AND HOPE FOR THE ALCOHOLIC

Help & Hope
for the Alcoholic

ALEXANDER C. DEJONG

Tyndale House
Publishers, Inc.
Wheaton, Illinois

Second printing, August 1983
Library of Congress Catalog Number 81-86092
ISBN 0-8423-1408-3
Copyright © 1982 by Alexander C. DeJong
Printed in the United States of America

CONTENTS

FOREWORD
11

PREFACE
13

ONE
One Sunday Morning
17

TWO
Facts and Fables
31

THREE
Overcoming Denial
45

FOUR
Unconditional Surrender
59

FIVE
In Touch with Self
73

SIX
In Touch with Others
85

SEVEN
In Touch with God
95

EIGHT
The Road Ahead
109

SELF-TEST FOR DRINKERS
119

SELF-TEST FOR FAMILY MEMBERS
121

RESOURCES
123

You give us many things that we pray for, and everything good that we receive before we pray we receive at your hands. I have never been a drunkard, but I have known drunkards who have been made sober by you. Therefore, it is your doing that some men have never been drunkards; it is your doing that others who have been drunkards should not always remain so; and it is also your doing that both sorts of men should know that it is your doing.

The Confessions of St. Augustine 10.31

[Christ] has fully paid for all my sins with his precious blood, and has set me free from the tyranny of the devil. He also watches over me in such a way that not a hair can fall from my head without the will of my Father in heaven: in fact, all things must work together for my salvation.

Heidelberg Catechism, A. 1

FOREWORD

God promises in the Book of Proverbs that the "path of life leads upward for the wise, to keep him from going down to the grave." On behalf of patients in my practice, my profession, and my church, I have been searching for wisdom about families marred by the disease of alcoholism. I search on behalf of the families in my practice because so many are affected and the results are so grave. I search on behalf of my profession because most doctors have no hope for the alcoholic and refuse to treat the illness. I search on behalf of my church because the attitudes present in churches and in their pastors' studies are many times no better than in the hospitals and the doctors' offices.

In addition, I search personally because, as with most families, there are those close to me who suffer from this disease.

My search has led me to a small group of individuals in my practice near Chicago, Illinois. Where I, my profession, and my church lacked wisdom, members of this group were living it. They were recovering alcoholics. They taught me the simple but difficult art of living through the twelve steps of their program. They were breathing testimonies to a path of life that led upward, some of them from very close to the grave.

The twelve steps of Alcoholics Anonymous (AA) contained much wisdom for the patients and the doctors, but one question still remained for me as a Christian physician: "Is there wisdom in this program for the Christian?"

That question is clearly addressed in the following pages. Among the many patients I've treated for alcoholism is this pastor who, after three decades of successful ministry, came to grips with his own illness.

Out of Pastor DeJong's struggle against this disease has come this book. I urge you to listen carefully as you read.

Martin Doot, M.D.
Medical Director, Alcoholic Treatment Center
MacNeal Memorial Hospital
Berwyn, Illinois
July 1981

PREFACE

"Tradition Twelve" of Alcoholics Anonymous (AA) claims that "[a]nonymity is the spiritual foundation of all our traditions, ever reminding us to place principles before personalities." Anonymity is thereby made a virtue in AA.

It began as a necessity. In the early days of AA, alcoholics were accustomed to hiding. In public, they were subject to distrust and contempt. The era of American prohibition had just ended, and the shame of lawlessness was easily attached to all forms of alcoholism. The foreword to the book which in 1939 first popularized Alcoholics Anonymous (known among AA members today as "the big book") explained, "It is important that we remain anonymous because we are too few, at present, to handle the overwhelming number of personal appeals which may result from this publication. Being mostly business or professional folk, we could not well carry on our occupations in such an event."

As a Christian, I have come to distrust anonymity. God knows us by name. Where can we hide? Since he accepts us as we are, why should we fear non-acceptance on the part of others?

Yet it is not easy to be open, to "come clean," to admit openly our powerlessness over alcohol. For a time I considered writing anonymously from behind a pseudonym. Some sincere friends suggested it would be better especially for a pastor to remain discreet.

But, while deeply appreciating such well-meant advice, I've chosen to identify my experiences with my name, and to share both with the broader Christian community. I do so out of concern for the countless Christian alcoholics who are today both hurting and hiding. I am constrained to witness openly to Christ's healing in my own life. Through sometimes painful steps toward recovery I have discovered liberation. With many thousands of recovering alcoholics I have learned to sing again,

> O give thanks to the Lord, for he is good;
> for his steadfast love endures forever!
> Let the redeemed of the Lord say so,
> whom he has redeemed from trouble.

[Ps. 107:1, 2, RSV]

One wins a race by taking a single step at a time. My journey to victory will be no different. The entire program of Alcoholics Anonymous is structured according to that conviction and consists in a series of "twelve steps" which one takes from alcoholism to freedom. I am profoundly grateful for this program. I view it as a tool wielded by the hand of God, one which ought to be sought out by every alcoholic.

My doctors and counselors have been especially skillful in introducing me to AA. Still, I believe it is Christ dwelling in my life who gave healing love to this program. He spoke and still speaks to me, even through the lives of some who have not yet experienced the power of the cross and resurrection. "Working the program" daily under the direction of Christ's Spirit will certainly lead to victory over alcoholism. That is my conviction, as well as my prayer.

I would especially like to acknowledge A. James Heynen who encouraged me to publish this book and to attach my real name to it rather than hide behind a pseudonym. As well, his editing of the early manuscript helped shape the book you are about to read.

Some of the material in chapter 2 owes a debt to Chaplain William Lenters, who, a couple of years ago, served as the executive secretary of Calvary Rehabilitation Center in Phoenix,

Arizona. Especially in the early months of recovery, his wise counsel helped me along the way of healing. At his invitation I went to Phoenix, Arizona, and for the first time shared publicly with the friends of Calvary Rehabilitation Center the many pains of my bondage and the joys of Christian recovery.

Like the Samaritan leper of gospel fame, I rejoice at hearing Christ say today, "Go your way; your faith has made you well" (Luke 17:19, RSV). Yet I hasten to add: Not my faith, Lord, but your grace.

A. C. DeJong

ONE
ONE SUNDAY
MORNING

I was brought low, and he helped me. Psalm 116:6, KJV

I am a Christian, a pastor, and an alcoholic.

After thirty years of ministry in the pulpit, I wrote the following to my church congregation:

> I am in MacNeal Memorial Hospital in Berwyn, Illinois, having fully accepted the fact that I have the disease of alcoholism. I have voluntarily submitted myself to the total program of the alcohol treatment center under the direction of a competent staff of doctors, counselors, and nurses. My family joins me in requesting your prayers that our Savior may place his healing hand upon my life.

At first I was frightened and helpless. I hadn't any idea how my congregation would react to my announcement; if anything, I expected rejection. I had signed myself into a detoxification ward, a place I'd advised others to go to many times, yet a place I myself had never been to before. Now that I was there, I desperately didn't want to be there.

But as I wrote my announcement, I felt an intense, serene sense of relief. A fresh calm infused every corner of my being. Guilt began to dissolve. Black clouds of depression slowly lifted.

My dark secret had been made public. I had finally faced the fact that I had the disease of alcoholism—a disease shared with 10 million other Americans—and I had finally admitted that fact to my friends and relatives. More remarkably, I had even admitted it to myself.

I am in MacNeal Hospital in Berwyn, Illinois, having fully accepted the fact that I have the disease of alcoholism.

The first sentence is always the hardest. This one was nearly impossible. It could be written only because it was so undeniably true. But at the same time I was coming to grips with this reality, other new insights were breaking through.

You see, I had been wrestling with the dilemma that is at the very core of alcoholism. Is it sin or is it sickness? For the longest time, I believed it was sin; I was responsible for my own suffering.

To many Christians, especially those that drink socially, this is a common way of thinking. They deal with alcohol entirely in terms of personal self-control, willpower, and moral discipline. To them, an alcoholic should know better than to drink at the wrong time or excessively. Certainly, then, when people drink too much or become alcoholic, they are committing a sin; they are failing to control their appetite for alcohol.

At one time this was the view I held. I believed that to see alcoholism as a disease would absolve people of personal responsibility and weaken our Christian view of what sin is.

But what I began to understand—as I confessed my own alcoholism and joined with others who confessed theirs—is that this view is simplistic and likely to do more damage than good. I myself was an example: as long as I believed that alcoholism was a sin, I tried to "will" myself out of it; I tried again and again to exercise self-discipline and personal control. In short, I attempted to beat it myself, when what I really needed was help from the outside. Finally, as I began to understand that alcoholism had *changed* me physically and psychologically—when I gradually came to accept that alcoholism was a disease—only then did I seek outside help. Only then could I be restored.

I have since turned more and more to the view that alcoholism is a disease, an illness, a physiological and psychological dependence beyond a person's control.

Sure, there is always an element of personal responsibility. And we can look at the widespread social epidemic of alcoholism and pronounce that it represents the effects of sin in the world. Alcoholism certainly is an evil and is the manifestation of sinfulness. But when this is brought down to the individual level, when we look into the distant, glazed eyes of an alcoholic, we see the ravages of a disease that has marched out of control. That soul whom God loves is not choosing to be what he is. He is a victim.

Now, I am not an expert on alcoholism. I have no authoritative pronouncements to give. I've not walked far enough down this new and sometimes difficult road to assume the right of expertise. But I've begun a second pilgrimage in life. And the new beginning has taught me six lessons which are worth considering.

1. No one knows the cause of alcoholism. It's a cunning, baffling, powerful disorder. It's an illness which invades the physical, emotional, intellectual, social, and spiritual dimensions of its victims.

Consider this: Two people may drink the same quantity of alcohol over a period of time. Person A's patterns of drinking remain constant and controlled. Person B begins to drink with a compulsive need. She increases intake. She begins to think ahead, to plan the next drink. Her sense of well-being is maintained only with a certain level of alcohol in her bloodstream. Person B now drinks alcoholically, while Person A remains a controlled, well-disciplined drinker—perhaps even with a quantitative intake greater than that of the "alcoholic." It isn't a matter of how much a person drinks, but simply *how* one drinks.

When did Person B become an alcoholic and why? Where is the line that Person B crossed, leaving behind controlled intake and crossing over to addiction? At what point did she enter the world of compulsive addictive drinking?

We don't know. And that's the point. While in some cases there may be an active, conscious, *sinful* choice to cross that line, more often than not that line is crossed before the person knows it. Furthermore, the person who believes he is drinking responsibly—that is, not sinning—may find himself one day miserably addicted to alcohol.

2. *The judgment of friends and relatives powerfully affects the choices of the alcoholic.* The last thing most alcoholics need is a stronger sense of guilt. This is especially true for Christian alcoholics: most of them pray for forgiveness more frequently, urgently, and sincerely than most observers will ever know. The greatest needs of the alcoholic are likely to be hope, acceptance, understanding, and assurance of forgiveness. Veiled and sometimes insensitive judgment on the part of those who reject the disease concept of alcoholism can and often does lead to further tragic injury for wounded Christians already caught in the trap of this sickness. If one rejects the illness approach, it is nonetheless urgent to recall that the causes of addiction are so varied, so ill-defined that true Christian concern recommends quiet reservation and strong, accepting patience.

3. *When an alcoholic is in the stage of denial, it is futile to argue with him the question of whether alcoholism is a sin or a sickness.* It is true—a practicing alcoholic may use the disease argument to justify his lifestyle. "I just can't help myself," he says. Some alcoholics love to argue and argue this issue— endlessly. As long as one is arguing, there's no need to stop drinking.

This is his frustrating pattern of denial. An alcoholic in this stage will be proud, clever, stubborn, deceptive, and sincere. Sincerity makes all the other characteristics hard to identify.

What it comes down to is this: argumentation can't be expected to cap an alcoholic's bottle. Christian friends would do better to seek practical ways to help the alcoholic achieve sobriety and victory. The Christian's best approach is understanding, patience, and love. Remember that help can be found in Christ, for he alone is both the forgiver of sin and the healer of all our diseases.

4. *Every Christian should be wary of the subtle, lethal poison of religious pride.* Some of those (though not all) who argue *against* the idea of alcoholism as disease may be guilty of the sin of pride. There are times when this argument holding alcoholics accountable for their sin sounds very much like the Pharisee's

prayer, "God, I thank thee, that I am not as other men . . ." (Luke 18:11, KJV).

Remember, no one chooses to become an alcoholic. I certainly did not. There is a very real sense in which alcoholism is something that "happened to" me but did not happen to my friends who drank with me. Therefore, my counsel to non-alcoholics who drink is: Take heed, lest you fall. Accept chemical independence as a gift from God. To the recovering alcoholic I suggest: Enjoy sobriety with thanksgiving. Thank God for this gift, recognizing that your healing comes each day, each hour, each minute not from human willpower or personal resources. This, like all health, comes from God.

5. *Accepting alcoholism as a disease creates an atmosphere conducive to healing.* When the alcoholic, his or her friends and family, and the Christian community approach the problem of alcoholism with understanding and compassion rather than condemnation and guilt, then alcoholics are more readily restored.

6. *There are stages in the progression of alcoholism, but one is just as much an alcoholic in the first stage as in the last stage.* The danger is to measure the severity of alcoholism by the appearance of the alcoholic. Alcoholism is like a street built on a hill and lined with a variety of homes. An alcoholic may move from the stately mansion near the top of the hill (first stage) to a seamy shack near the bottom of the hill (last stage). But he or she is just as alcoholic in one as in the other. In fact, most alcoholics are living toward the top of the hill (only 5 percent of alcoholics are of the skid-row variety). So, alcoholism may sometimes be hard for nonalcoholics to discern; what's worse, it can be easy for alcoholics to rationalize, especially if they are in the early stages of the disease.

I believe that alcoholism is both sin *and* sickness. As an alcoholic I am both a responsible sinner and a nonresponsible victim. I am *responsible* for my actions and at the same time *victimized* by what alcohol does to me. I experience helplessness, and yet I have willed myself into helplessness. I have willfully sinned, but I cannot will myself out of the tangle of sin in which I am ensnared.

21

Perhaps this diagram will help illustrate what I mean:

ALCOHOLISM

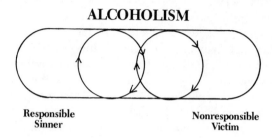

**Responsible
Sinner**

**Nonresponsible
Victim**

The ellipse or elongated oval is entitled alcoholism. In the ellipse are two circles. Each circle revolves around its own center. The center of the left circle is denoted *responsible sinner.* The center of the right circle is denoted *nonresponsible victim.* The left circle represents ideas, thoughts, feelings, desires, decisions, and choices for which the person is responsible. He acts by choice. The right circle represents ideas, thoughts, feelings, desires, decisions, choices for which the person is not responsible. He is victimized by his sickness. Each circle is in rotating motion. Each circle moves within the other. They mesh and intersect in a manner so complex and blurred that it is impossible to draw clear lines at the points where the non-responsible victim becomes a responsible sinner, or the responsible (choosing) sinner becomes an enslaved victim. The alcoholic remains a unique and impenetrable combination of freedom and bondage.

The alcoholic needs to walk the road of victory in Jesus Christ. It is each alcoholic's personal, special responsibility to seek this way immediately. The path over Calvary and past the empty tomb is the only hope for total redemption from the terror of alcoholism.

But many active alcoholics who are Christians remain hopelessly caught in the snare of their illness because they (and the Christian community which surrounds them) feel that their sickness is sin. Overwhelmed by guilt, they feel isolated, ashamed, fearful, and abandoned. Often their fellow Christians have no idea of alcoholics' anguish. It is only open, sympathetic, and insightful conversation on this complicated issue which will help many hidden Christian alcoholics to come out from behind the painful security of hiding and hurt.

The American Medical Association defines alcoholism like this: "Alcoholism is a chronic, progressive, and potentially fatal disease. It is characterized by tolerance and physical dependency or pathologic organ changes, or both—all the direct or indirect consequences of the alcohol ingested."

It is safe to say that when a person's drinking interferes with the religious, professional, social, emotional, or physical aspects of his life, he or she is either an alcoholic or definitely on the way to becoming one. As a sickness alcoholism has an identifiable constellation of symptoms. The eight symptoms which are discussed below are those most frequently mentioned in literature on alcoholism, which is widely available at local hospitals, mental health clinics, Alcoholics Anonymous meetings, or public libraries.

1. *The alcoholic thinks about drinking a great deal of the time.* Preoccupation with alcohol is the key symptom. The alcoholic plans his life around alcohol. He will eat or socialize only where alcohol is served or fortify himself at home or at a bar if he foresees a long dry spell.

2. *The alcoholic possesses a high tolerance for the drug alcohol.* Early on the "pleasant" road to bondage he is able to drink more than others without apparent ill effect.

3. *The alcoholic sneaks and gulps drinks.* He or she may offer to function as host or hostess in order to imbibe a couple of drinks more than are being served to the guests. The alcoholic needs more alcohol to achieve the desired state of euphoria than the controlled social drinker.

4. *The alcoholic often drinks alone.* Christian alcoholics particularly are often very cautious about their intake in public. They may be careful to buy booze where they will not be seen. They drink in the privacy of their own homes.

5. *The alcoholic uses drink to relieve tension and anxiety.* He often uses Paul's "a little wine for the stomach's sake" to justify compulsive need.

6. *The alcoholic may experience a blackout.* This is not a typical

passing-out because one's nerve centers have been anesthetized. It is rather a type of amnesia where a person who has been drinking appears to be functioning normally, but the next day he cannot remember what was said or done.

7. *The alcoholic protects and often hides the supply of alcohol.* One goes to great lengths and expense to make sure that a supply is always available. It becomes a source of serenity and courage.

8. *The alcoholic drinks at inappropriate times.* He drinks more than he planned to drink and at times when he did not expect to drink. Thereby he begins to exhibit a definite lack of control over where, when, and how much he drinks.

Most authorities agree that if a person exhibits four or more of the above eight symptoms with some regularity, there is little question that the sickness of alcoholism is present. There are simple questionnaires available to anyone who wants to take a personal inventory of his alcohol use.

There is a self-test included at the back of this book. Inventory yourself. The results may surprise you.

I have voluntarily submitted myself. . . .

Every alcoholic is both sick and responsible for seeking help. He must acknowledge that the illness—which was, at least in the beginning, self-induced—is wrong, and that to set himself right he needs assistance. But it is not merely a "turning away from," it is also a "turning to." The drinking alcoholic has learned to look for hope at the bottom of a bottle. To turn away from the bottle requires the conviction that there is hope elsewhere. And there is.

There are legions of people trained to help control this progressive and chronic illness. They stand ready to assist twenty-four hours each day across North America. All that's required of the alcoholic is a clear, sturdy decision to seek help, followed by a quick telephone call or visit.

But therein lies a difficulty. A basic symptom of the disease itself is this: alcoholics are increasingly robbed of their capacity to make sharp, firm decisions. As dependence on alcohol increases, the ability to act swiftly, to make decisions without reservations, decreases. Alcoholics are content to drift, to deny, to coast.

Nonaction is attractive, easy, comfortable. The next manhattan or martini makes postponement not only possible but downright pleasurable.

Victory over this disease can come only when an alcoholic's denial—the source of infinite delay—disappears and the person sincerely recognizes that the point of surrender has come. With alcoholism as with the Christian faith, to become strong one must confess utter weakness; to be rescued, one must give up trying to save oneself.

> *. . . to the total program of the alcoholic treatment center. . . .*

One dimension of the alcoholism tragedy is that the disease is so wonderfully treatable. The sometimes fatal prejudice—once a drunk, always a drunk—is simply not true. Alcoholism is most certainly curable, and there are thousands and thousands of persons meeting together weekly who are living testimonies to one another of that fact.

Most communities in the United States and Canada are located near some facility for the treatment of addictions, including alcoholism. Nearly every city and town has a chapter of Alcoholics Anonymous meeting weekly (check your telephone directory). Since alcoholism has become recognized as the third largest health problem in North America, treatment centers and other sources of help have grown not only in number but also in effectiveness.

A typical alcoholism treatment center now provides physical examinations, full medical care, psychological testing, individual counseling and group therapy, lecture sessions about the disease itself, programs for reading and entertainment (something to take the place of bars, booze, and family rooms), and always, AA meetings. In Christian treatment centers, a Spirit-led dimension of spiritual counsel and support is added to such programs.

A painful lesson learned by many alcoholics in treatment programs is that one must go all the way and work the program every day. The *total program* must be accepted. As in other areas of life, alcoholics in treatment often dislike most intensely the phase of rehabilitation which they need most.

My family joins me in requesting your prayers. . . .

Alcoholism is a family disease. Not a single family member can escape its devastating power. It stunts the growth of love, clogs the channels of communication, makes ugly what God made beautiful. When a husband or wife, parent or child, becomes an alcoholic, no one in the family can avoid the agony inflicted through this wretched illness.

But family support can be a powerful incentive to move the alcoholic out of denial and into surrender. More than any others, sensitive, caring members of my own family were used by Christ to bring me to his healing. I discovered new-born meaning in the words of Psalm 128:3, 4: "Your wife will be like a fruitful vine within your house; your children will be like olive shoots around your table. Lo, thus shall the man be blessed who fears the Lord" (RSV).

When intimacy steadily soured into isolation, my wife refused to quit. Like many others, she "covered" for me. She was sure I had only cultivated a bad habit. She offered excuses for me, intending only to diminish my pain. Surely, she thought, her husband's willpower would be able to break the hold of mere alcohol. It took years for this illusion to dissolve, for her to face the terrible truth that good intentions and sincere efforts had only helped me hide from the reality that I was sick. But eventually her own efforts at denial ended. It was undeniable at last that her husband was not a naughty boy caught in a bad habit. He was an alcoholic who needed healing, not hiding; care, not condemnation.

Once she had grasped that fact, not a worthwhile pamphlet or book on alcoholism in the local library was left unread. She studied and prayed, prayed and studied. The more she realized her husband suffered an illness, the less pain and frustration she experienced. She confronted her own feelings of guilt and despair. Eventually it was she who, strengthened by Christ's Spirit, steadied my soul as well as my hand as I wrote my note to the congregation. For the first time in years, her prayers were openly, fully fused with mine.

Our "olive shoots" had left the table years before. They had homes of their own. But they knew from clinical experience what alcoholism is and does (all three are medical doctors). More important than what they knew was that they *cared*. Their training in ATCs (Alcohol Treatment Centers) had equipped them with professional expertise. But it was their love, not merely their skill, which brought our three sons to support their mother and me. With tender, persistent, tough love they compelled me to face reality. In their silences as well as our conversations I could feel their affection. And when the time came for this note of confession to be read to the 600 members of my congregation, my sons walked down the church aisle and took their customary places, giving unembarrassed support to their parents.

On that Sunday morning I knew the support of my wife and children. But I was unsure how God's family, the church, would react. What would be said? Would there be criticism and hostility? Would there be the knowing glances which meant "I told you so"? Worse, would there be laughter? For a very long time I had hidden my condition out of fear; at the core of that fright was the nightmare of this moment when I would be exposed. Like every other member of my congregation I had grown up believing that alcoholics are weak and morally inferior. Only compelling fear and the sure promises of God enabled me to endure this moment.

God sometimes provides what we cannot even imagine. Instead of hostility, telephone calls—some over long distances—brought messages of support and encouragement within hours of the reading of my note. There were promises of prayer and gifts of hope and cheerfulness. Oh, there were some disappointments: some people I hoped would call remained silent. But many people I never imagined would care offered kindnesses in ways too private to publish. The age-old "communion of the saints" sprang to life with fresh dimensions of personal meaning. The little note read publicly, forged in the privacy of pain and intimacy of family love, triggered a release of Christian love too precious to tarnish with inadequate descriptions.

> . . . *that our strong Savior may place his healing hand upon my life.*

Christ uses all kinds of hands as his own to bring healing. As I carry on my work helping fellow alcoholics, I hold hands with many at AA meetings as we conclude with a recitation of the Lord's Prayer. Many of these praying alcoholics are not confessing Christians. Some left the organized church because they felt ashamed, guilty, and unwelcome. A few have never been church members. Most are not anti-Christian. A few may be covert Christians, or even "pre-Christians." God knows their pasts and their futures, and God knows they are sick.

These delightful, religiously complicated people, content to pray the Lord's Prayer only at an AA meeting, always listen respectfully when I witness to the healing power of Christ. My studies in the Scriptures taught me long ago that Christ uses many words of unlikely people in surprising places to work his miracles of salvation. That truth has been underscored in my own recent experiences as God used people too numerous to count to aid in his rescue of me. I take this opportunity to thank them publicly and to praise the Lord who used them in my life.

And I say this in the first chapter of my story because it needs to be heard loudly and distinctly in the community of Christians who know so little about alcoholism and AA and AA's related programs. Christ is present and busy in hospitals. He is at work in group therapy sessions where some of the language used is not fit for the streets, let alone appropriate to the pulpit. He visits small chapels and moves along narrow, dark sidewalks. He can be found in late-night conversations in many parked cars. His presence brings sobriety, freedom, and love in thousands of unexpected ways.

In my own life and ministry I fear I've been guilty of trying to box in the Lord. I've sometimes joined with others who wanted to confine him to the box labeled "church." We've sought to define him with a theological formula and limit him with our sentimental stories. But Christ has wonderful ways of exploding from our little boxes tied with religious ribbons. His ways *are* higher than our ways. His thoughts *are* bigger than our thoughts. He is able to find those who have not even sought him out (Isa. 65:1). When members of the afflicted community at an AA meeting join hands and begin together, "Our Father who art in heaven," that Father is being addressed by those whom he has healed. It is to that incomparable truth that I witness in such settings. Where alcoholics have been set at liberty, it is by Christ's stripes that they are healed—even if they do not (yet) know that it is he who has healed them.

TWO
FACTS AND FABLES

And ye shall know the truth, and the truth shall make you free.
John 8:32, KJV

An alcoholic takes his or her first step toward recovery when facing facts for what they are: facts. While living in the make-believe world of "I can handle it," I was unable to take that step. Without the pain of confronting life honestly, I could not openly admit my powerlessness. I had learned to see the world through the bottom of a bottle, and I no longer recognized reality from any other perspective. I needed to separate facts from fables, truth from tales, and knowledge from mythology. Looking back now, I realize that my struggle was common to all alcoholics. Winning over alcoholism involves, I believe, three things: knowing what your drinking is all about, understanding who you really are, and believing what Christ is willing to do through your working the twelve steps of Alcoholics Anonymous.

There are probably enough myths about alcoholism to fill a standard library. You've probably heard most of them yourself:

> I drink only beer. No hard stuff for me. I can't be an alcoholic.

> I never drink in the morning, and I never drink when I'm alone. I couldn't be an alcoholic.

> I can quit anytime.

31

These are the normal defenses of "typical" alcoholics, and they're based on nothing but the mythology of alcoholism. While those myths may be nothing more than silly misunderstandings or forgivable ignorance for nonalcoholics, they are tragic when alcoholics begin to believe the myths and use them to keep drinking.

This chapter concerns the mythology of alcoholism. It's included because anyone seriously interested in aiding alcoholics toward recovery must have more than good intent and Christian hope: those who are most helpful are those who have solid knowledge.

Test yourself. Are the following statements true or false?

1. Before he can provide help, a counselor must first discover *why* an alcoholic drinks.

    False. Once a person has contracted an addiction, the reasons for his addiction are of little importance. Alcoholics drink because they are alcoholics. Learning the reasons why a person began drinking (or using other drugs) in the first place may be important in order to prevent a relapse, but once the disease is present, worrying about why it happened is as useless as if a home owner, watching his house burn, asked why it started. The cure for a blazing house is to call the fire department and douse the fire. The cure for alcoholism is to stop drinking.

2. Psychiatry is the best treatment for alcoholism.

    False. Alcoholics Anonymous has had the most notable success in alcoholism treatment. AA attacks the alcoholism itself, rather than any underlying problems which may or may not be present. Other more recent programs based upon the AA model (Overeaters Anonymous, Emotions Anonymous, Gamblers Anonymous, etc.) are also meeting with remarkable success throughout the country.

3. Many social drinkers do not become alcoholic.

    True. Although the causes of alcoholism or addiction of any kind are largely unknown, it is fairly certain that some kind of "X-factor" is necessary before the disease can develop. That factor may be genetic, biochemical, or may spring from another cause.

4. Some social drinkers can suddenly become alcoholic without realizing it.

True. A sudden and traumatic experience such as forced retirement or the death of a loved one can trigger alcoholic drinking in the life of a social drinker. Statistical studies have demonstrated the relationship.

5. The reason alcoholics don't cut down or stop drinking is because they have weak characters and lack willpower.

False. I completely accepted this myth for a long time. Willpower and strength of character can neither cause nor cure a disease. Character development may be a factor in preventing a relapse, but there is little evidence to prove even this. Efforts to control drinking by willpower alone can aggravate the alcoholic's problem. Willpower has as little to do with the disease of alcoholism as it does with heart disease. One cannot will to be rid of the disease of alcoholism.

6. Nearly 90 percent of all alcoholics are middle-aged, homeless men.

False. About 3 percent of all people with alcoholism fall into this category. Ninety-seven percent of all alcoholics are persons raising families, holding jobs, struggling to do their best to function in the face of a killer disease. Unfortunately they usually have little knowledge or understanding of the true nature of their crippling bondage.

7. A bad marriage and poor family relationships can cause alcoholism in a family member.

False. No person can cause alcoholism in another. Although they often feel unwarranted guilt, neither the spouse, the children, nor the alcoholic is to blame. Just as no person begins using alcohol to become alcoholic, so no one causes alcoholism in another person either.

8. A normal person can avoid becoming an alcoholic by drinking moderately.

   False. This is a popular fable in communities long on Christian liberty and short on Christian training. I believed this fable for a long time. Many otherwise normal persons develop alcoholism after even light and infrequent drinking.

9. Most active members of AA recover successfully.

   True. Although relapse is a part of this disease, a recent survey by AA indicates about a 79 percent recovery rate for active members who maintain two continuous years of sobriety, and a 91 percent recovery rate for those members who have been sober for five years.

10. Alcoholism cuts across all social and economic classes.

    True. So does cancer, heart disease, diabetes, and tooth decay. Alcoholism is an equal opportunity disease. Recovery, too, cuts across all social and economic classes.

11. Most alcoholics seem to be unusually sensitive to the attitudes of others.

    True. On the surface, it may not appear so. In reality, however, it is often sensitivity to the judgmental and moralistic attitudes of family, friends, and professionals that causes denial of the problem. People in pain are always sensitive to the attitudes of others, and people suffering from self-condemnation are usually extrasensitive.

12. Passing out is the same as blacking out.

    False. One of the most misunderstood symptoms of alcoholism, the blackout, is simply a drug-induced memory loss. It has nothing to do with passing out. It is an occasion when the victim appears to function normally, but is later unable to recall events. Blackouts can last from a few seconds to a few days, and do not require severe intoxication to occur. For example, after drinking, a person may drive home, arrive there safely, but the next morning be unable to recall how he or she got home. That is a blackout.

13. Alcoholics must ask for treatment before it will be effective.

     False. Ninety percent of the people in treatment entered treatment under duress of some kind. For me it was the blessed but painful pressure of Christ which sent me to the hospital. Most loudly deny that alcohol is a problem for them. It is the job of the treatment center to help the person break through delusion and see the reality of alcoholism in his life. It is the responsibility of those of us who are healthy—family, friends, employers, co-workers, ministers, doctors—to get the individual to treatment. Do not expect the person with a drug-affected mind to make wise decisions regarding his future. That alcoholics must voluntarily seek treatment before it can help is probably the most damaging myth of all! How long would you wait to suggest to someone dear that an obvious illness needs treatment? The rationalization-and-denial system of the alcoholic makes it mandatory that family and friends find ways to assist the victim to treatment. Since in today's society having a drinking problem still involves some moral and social stigma, many alcoholics should not be expected to admit their illness voluntarily.

14. Alcoholism is a self-inflicted disease.

     False. Why would anyone choose to inflict a disease as ugly, painful, and destructive as this one upon himself? Even if such infliction were possible, the very idea that over 10 million people would *choose* alcoholism is ludicrous.

15. A spouse must sometimes create a crisis by leaving the home before the alcoholic will accept help.

     True. Often, in counseling, I now suggest that those concerned use alcohol-induced crisis incidents as leverage to move the alcoholic toward accepting treatment. Such a careful, nonjudgmental recitation of what has happened because of his drinking often becomes indisputable proof to the alcoholic that he has a problem. Called the "tough love" concept, this is a technique that can be taught to willing family members, employers, and others. It is also sometimes called "confrontation without condemnation."

16. Family members other than the alcoholic also need a treatment-and-recovery program.

    True. As I said earlier, alcoholism is a family disease. Living with alcoholism will, over a very short period of time, create emotional problems for the other victims of alcoholism. These emotional and psychological problems require treatment. Family treatment is the best form of prevention available. Did you know that a very high percentage (50-85 percent) of the untreated children of alcoholics will themselves develop alcoholism?

17. How often, how much, and when a person drinks are the important things to know in order to determine if someone has alcoholism.

    False. It's not how much a person drinks, what time of day, or how often, that determines the presence of alcoholism. The basic question here is "What is alcohol doing to the drinker's life?" Amount and time of consumption prove little. Many alcoholics drink only sporadically, and many social drinkers consume quantities of alcohol far beyond the tolerance of some persons with alcoholism.

18. A definite cause has been established for alcoholism.

    False. No one cause nor even several potential causes combined have been isolated to tell us why some people contract alcoholism and others do not. When an absolute cause is found, perhaps prevention and cure will be more readily accessible.

19. Alcohol has the same chemical and psychological effect on everyone who drinks.

    False. Many individual and basic differences in psychological and physical reactions have been documented.

20. Tranquilizers, such as Librium or Valium, help keep alcoholics from drinking.

    False. The so-called "minor" tranquilizers, as well as most other sedative or mood-altering drugs, can be dangerous additions to the problems of chemically dependent persons. The sense of well-being created by these drugs will often lead to relapse, with multiple addiction (being "hooked" on both alcohol and other drugs) as the tragic result.

21. Alcoholics are harder to work with and help than most other patients, and attempts to help them are usually unsuccessful.
    False. No one has the power to judge that another person is beyond help. Recovery from alcoholism can and does occur at all stages in the disease. Like other diseases, it is more easily treated in its early stages, but middle- and even late-stage recoveries are not uncommon. Further, with today's more sophisticated treatment facilities and techniques, the prognosis for recovery can be excellent. It was the Lord Jesus Christ working through these means who brought liberating healing into my own life.

22. People who drink only beer rarely develop alcoholism.
    False. Twelve ounces of beer, five ounces of wine, or one and one-half ounces of distilled spirits may have different volume, but they share the same amount of alcohol. Many alcoholics have been fooled by the myth that "You can't be alcoholic if you drink only beer." Don't believe it.

23. Alcoholics are generally good employees.
    True. Over 95 percent of the people with alcoholism are struggling to function daily on their jobs and in their homes. Many alcoholic people make heroic efforts to hold on to their jobs, forcing themselves to be better and more reliable workers than other employees as a way of compensating for their illness.

24. Someone who drinks only on weekends cannot be classified as alcoholic.
    False. Many alcoholics drink only on weekends. For most, the weekend eventually extends into the rest of the week, but the process may take years. Weekend or "binge" alcoholism usually does severe physical and emotional damage to the alcoholic and his or her family.

25. Al-Anon and Alateen are for female and young alcoholics.
    False. Al-Anon is an organization similar to AA, but one

which helps all adult family members and other persons concerned (male or female) understand alcoholism and their feelings about themselves and the alcoholic person. Alateen is a companion organization for the children (twelve years to eighteen years) of alcoholic persons.

26. Alcoholics and their families often complain to social workers, doctors, and others about problems *un*related to drinking but never mention that drinking is involved.
    True. Frequently, the alcoholic and his or her family are unaware that alcoholism is causing the problem. Sometimes attempts to solve other problems without mentioning alcohol are part of the denial inherent in the disease. Spouses become as involved in their own denial as the alcoholic. This is especially so among Christians who associate alcoholism with moral inferiority.

27. The drug Antabuse can cure alcoholism if taken faithfully.
    False. Antabuse (disulfiram) provides a temporary crutch to curb an impulse to drink. For long-term recovery, however, the patient must learn to live and value a drug-free life. No cure for alcoholism exists. It can only be arrested and treated.

28. An alcoholic can learn new behavior patterns that will eventually permit a return to social drinking.
    False. A person whose body and mind have become addicted to drugs cannot safely return to the use of drugs. With appropriate treatment, hundreds of thousands of people are finding a chemical-free life to be far more rewarding than a return to the use of alcohol and other drugs. Long experience has shown that attempts to return to drinking or using other drugs, no matter how long the individual has been drug-free, are nearly always disastrous.

29. In treatment, education about alcoholism is meaningless.
    False. Much of the treatment for both the alcoholic and his or her family consists of education. Although

knowledge will not cure this disease, it can help prevent
or shorten a relapse. Education often may motivate the
alcoholic to seek help. It did in my life.

30. Some type of painful crisis is usually necessary before the
alcoholic will seek help.

True. A painful crisis is usually necessary in order to break
through the chemical barrier of defenses, rationalization,
and denial the alcoholic has created. Remember, the
alcoholic's thinking is drug-affected and not likely to be
rational even when he or she is relatively sober. The
alcoholic may appear rational in many discussions: he or
she may argue coherently, speak clearly, explain patiently;
but when it comes to the perception of alcohol and its use,
he or she loses perspective and is closed to help. The
alcoholic has effectively, often unconsciously, blocked out
the idea that a real problem exists. Feeling the full impact
of a painful crisis may permit such a person to begin
realizing the seriousness of his or her illness. Family and
friends will often force crises for the alcoholic in the name
of love, for example, a wife may threaten to leave her
alcoholic husband if he doesn't seek help, thereby
inducing pain to initiate healing.

31. Alcoholics are prone to addiction to any mood-altering drug.

True. While certain sedative or mood-altering drugs may
be relatively safe for some persons, people who are
alcoholic almost always can develop an addiction to such
drugs. It is very important that these drugs be prescribed
for alcoholics only under controlled conditions and
competent medical supervision.

32. Recovering alcoholics should always avoid visiting places
where liquor is being served.

False. In today's society, avoiding liquor is almost
impossible. The recovering alcoholic must learn to live
comfortably in a drinking society. He deserves to be
afforded the dignity of making his own choices. Hiding
liquor from an alcoholic, recovering or not, is both
insulting and futile.

33. Alcoholism is a major cause of suicide.

    True. At least one third of all suicides are alcohol related. This gives the lie to the image of "good-time Charlie." Alcoholism is not fun, no matter how comic the appearance of the victim.

34. To be a genuine alcoholic, the person must drink at least every day or two.

    False. It is fairly easy for most alcoholics to abstain completely for varying periods of time, even for years. However, an untreated or "dry" alcoholic is usually an unhappy person who expends great amounts of grim effort on staying dry. When that person drinks again, the alcoholic symptoms become progressively more severe. Introducing the chemical into the alcoholic's system quickly reactivates the viciously intense need for the drug. I experienced this phenomenon personally. I was "dry" for long periods, even up to a year. Yet I never lost my sense of painful bondage.

35. Pleading and reasoning will sometimes make an alcoholic stop drinking.

    False. One of the cruelest statements ever made by one human being to another is "If you really love me, you'll stop drinking." That's like saying to a tubercular, "If you love me, you'll stop coughing!" Pleading and reasoning simply add to the family's frustration, pain, and anger, and to the alcoholic's already overloaded sense of guilt. Such uninformed pleading and reasoning make it even more difficult for everyone who is in denial to seek treatment.

36. Probably the strongest suspicion that alcoholism is present is the fact that drinking causes problems in a person's life.

    True. When problems in any area of life—family, job, school, health, or with the law—repeatedly arise accompanied with the use of alcohol, alcoholism should be strongly suspected.

37. Only morally weak people catch the disease of alcoholism.

    False. Morally weak people develop alcoholism; so do

morally strong people and morally mediocre people. Alcoholism isn't choosy. It will strike anyone, regardless of morality. And the Christian never forgets his strong inclination to carnality. Romans 7 is a very expressive piece of revelation for him (Rom. 7:15—"For that which I do, I allow not: for what I would, that do I not; but what I hate, that do I").

38. Alcoholism is a progressive and treatable disease.
    True. Every major medical, psychiatric, and psychological association agreed with this statement more than twenty years ago. Continued debate on the point is useless. The fact is that whether you choose to believe the scientists or not, when alcoholism is treated in ways other than as a disease, alcoholics die and their families often deteriorate. Alcoholism is a disease. It is progressive. And—thank God—it is treatable.

39. Alcohol is a drug.
    True. Alcohol is a highly addictive, mood-altering, sedative-hypnotic drug, chemically similar to ether. It is probably the most seriously abused drug. Heroin, for example, creates fewer serious physical problems for fewer people. There are about 300,000 heroin addicts in the United States and 10 to 20 million alcohol addicts. Further, unsupervised withdrawal from alcohol is often fatal. Serious health problems, in addition to the well-known liver damage, result from alcohol abuse. Alcoholics are five times more prone to cancer than other people. Many causes of heart disease result from alcohol abuse. With heart disease and cancer, alcoholism is often listed as one of the "Big Three" health problems in America today.

40. Alcohol affects the judgment of alcoholics only.
    False. Alcohol affects the judgment and decision-making ability of everyone who drinks it. The first effect of the ingestion of alcohol is impaired judgment. It is consumed precisely for that feeling of "taking the edge off," or euphoria. It "helps" to cut down the pain level of so many meaningless lives.

41. When an alcoholic asks for help, it is best to wait a few days to see if he or she really means it.

    False. When an alcoholic asks for help, see that help is made available immediately. The person may not ask again for years—or ever.

42. Describing alcoholism as a disease downplays the Christian teaching of personal responsibility.

    False. The problem drinker is not responsible for catching the disease of alcoholism but is primarily responsible for the decisive and necessary steps to seek help.

If you've read the "catechism on alcoholism" above, you should have no problem with the following multiple-choice questions:

A person suffering from alcoholism is
    A. always drunk.
    B. unable to control how much he/she drinks.
    C. usually unemployed.
    D. often a "skid-row bum."
    E. all of the above.

B. The hallmark of alcoholism is that the victim is unable to predict consistently, to control, or to manage how much alcohol he or she will consume on any one drinking occasion. Social or normal drinkers rarely have this problem. Even small amounts of alcohol at inappropriate times or on improper occasions are a sure mark of alcoholism.

If you are intoxicated, the best **aid to** becoming sober is
    A. black coffee.
    B. a cold shower.
    C. time.
    D. vigorous exercise.
    E. all of the above.

C. Only allowing the body sufficient time to metabolize the alcohol will sober a person. All other time-worn remedies will simply produce a wide-awake drunk.

Which of the following describes the action of alcohol on the body?
   A. depressant.
   B. stimulant.
   C. both stimulant and depressant.
   D. neither a stimulant nor a depressant.
   E. none of the above.

C. Because of the initial euphoria, or well-being, people often use alcohol as a stimulant. It is, in fact, a depressant drug causing mental and physical depression in all users, not just alcoholics. Alcohol may act as a stimulant as long as a person keeps on drinking (often because the drinker is losing normal inhibitions). Depressant effects are experienced when alcohol intake stops or the crowd goes home.

Whether one is hooked on daily alcohol intake, grass-smoking euphoria, or soothing "peace" from overdosing the physician's prescription of Valium, every addict builds his or her defenses called *denial*. But this deadly weapon, wielded with creativity and ease, demands a chapter of its own.

THREE
OVERCOMING
DENIAL

He that trusteth in his own heart is a fool. Proverbs 28:26, KJV

Being a *pastor* is one thing. Being an *alcoholic* is another. Being an *alcoholic pastor* is something else again. But one of the earliest discoveries I made on the road to recovery was that alcoholics come in all sizes and shapes.

There are regular, respectable types, for example, who may have two or three martinis at lunch, a few more to unwind before dinner, and another two or three to ensure a good night's sleep. Another type, even more "respectable" (and usually unknown), does not drink daily but runs from reality into a bottle as many as three or four times a year. A third type regularly stops at his favorite "watering hole" because going home immediately after work to "the old lady and the kids" is such an unpleasant prospect. Then there is the loner who hides a bottle in her bedroom and lulls her hurts into insensibility. If you or someone close to you is an alcoholic, you can probably add to these descriptions of drinking patterns. They are legion. But common to each pattern is a neatly organized, impermeable shell of *denial.*

DENIAL
Denial is the most general and the most insidious factor in the disease called "alcoholism." By *denial* I mean *all the efforts the*

alcoholic makes to hide from conscious awareness the existence of his or her illness. Denial is the shield used to protect one's inner self from the truth. It is a devastatingly effective means of clinging to feelings of self-worth while effectively committing suicide ounce by ounce.

Denial is a demon with many faces. A person can simply lie about his drinking habits. In an offhanded manner, sometimes spiced with a witty quip or a handy grin, the alcoholic can minimize the amount as well as the bad effects of his drinking. Each alcoholic will convincingly state his own reasons for when and how much he drinks. His or her repertoire of excuses and alibis for drinking is infinite. In rationalizations, an alcoholic displays creativity, moral persuasiveness, and great plausibility. He denies that he is alcoholic while he intellectualizes about it. She may react in anger to questions about her drinking with a furious "Who, *me?* Who are *you* to talk?"

Every alcoholic invents those forms of denial which most effectively enable him or her to keep on drinking. I remember my own web of denial. And I remember how that web was finally swept away by a wave of heavy, searing pain under which I had no choice but to confess powerlessness over alcohol.

But if you are still actively denying your own alcoholism, these words may help you see how sick you really are. Pain—sharp and relentless pain—often opens the way to acceptance of personal powerlessness. It is often in despair that an alcoholic gets the first clear vision of how unmanageable life has actually become. Until that time, denial is maintained with a marvelous array of techniques usually built out of "rationalizations" and "projections."

Human beings use excuses to get rid of bad feelings and to build up good self-images. *Rationalization* is a fancy word for inventing acceptable explanations to justify one's unacceptable behavior. Everyone devises his own reasons. An alcoholic tries to defend drinking patterns to himself as well as to others. He or she always has a believable reason for drinking. During the denial phase of alcoholism, those reasons appear to be sensible, appropriate, and wonderfully innocent.

Reasoning may go like this:

I drink to relax. A couple of manhattans at bedtime will grant me a much-needed good night's sleep. Two martinis certainly are in order to release the tension and grief I feel over the loss of a loved one.

I need a bracer to face the cruel world which is so insensitive to my particular anxieties.

I drink because my business associates demand the sociability of a cocktail.

Everyone in the neighborhood takes a drink and I don't want to be a misfit.

An alcoholic drinks because he or she is misunderstood or underrated or abused or divorced or married or happy or sad or lonely or busy or excited or bored or depressed or. . . . The list is endless. Each problem drinker devises new reasons. But just behind carefully constructed rationalizations there cowers a pitiable person, frightened and hurting, who needs acceptance and early help to overcome the denial of his or her real status.

Projection is the act of assigning to others blame for one's own misdeeds. It's the "not me" syndrome which protects the vulnerable ego. As long as the alcoholic can place the blame for his or her situation on something, or someone, else—or even on some distant event or fear—drinking continues with relative ease. She will say that she drinks because of her husband. Perhaps it's a wife or parents or boss or church or police or judge or neighbors or kids; maybe it's the system. Maybe it's life. In each case, the sharp arrow of blame is aimed in any direction except toward one's own conduct.

Well-meaning friends and relatives often lend support to this kind of delusional thinking. In fact, clever drinkers may manipulate their friends and family so skillfully—loudly denying their problem and claiming to be wounded by such awful suggestions—that others feel guilty for bringing up the whole problem of alcoholism (or, as it's usually called at this stage, "heavy drinking").

Over the years, alcoholics have often been successful in conning their physicians into prescribing various tranquilizers. Then the liquid drug, alcohol, is joined or replaced by a dry drug such as Valium. Such tranquilizers only help reenforce the presence of denial. After all, now a physician also realizes that the alcoholic "needs" sedation. The doctor agrees and is "helping." Does it matter if I achieve serenity by the use of a pill or a drink, so long as the result is the same? The alcoholic stays out of touch with the pain of life. A strengthened denial system enables him or her to keep open the possibility of pleasant experiences with mood-altering drugs.

Denial works to preserve the perception of self-worth ("I'm OK; I can control my life!"). A doctor's unwitting participation bolsters the rationalization that a drug can help ease life's burdens. And as problems mount and suspicions deepen, the alcoholic deflects every question, every hint of trouble, with a fervent "Not *me!* It's the other person. I don't have a problem. I'm not an alcoholic. *My* case is entirely different."

DENYING AND DYING

The alcoholic denies having the disease of alcoholism much as some people deny the reality of their own impending deaths. It gradually became clear to me that my own denial of the disease of alcoholism was much like the stages a person may experience when facing death. Dr. Kubler-Ross, in *On Death and Dying*, describes the various attitudes toward death as follows:

1. *Denial and isolation.* The sick person barricades him or herself from the entrance of the enemy. This is usually done alone.
2. *Anger.* "It's not *me!*" "Why *me?*" "Not now. . . ." Such anger can be reasonable in its expression, but more often it is irrational.
3. *Bargaining.* One makes an agreement with God or another person of power. "If you heal me, I promise to pay you back by. . . ."
4. *Depression.* A fading smile is replaced with a heavy heart, a pessimistic attitude, a grey-black outlook.
5. *Acceptance.* For the Christian this is surrender into the hands of the One who defeated death. It can mean the beginning of real life.

The alcoholic is a person in the act of dying as certainly as the patient with terminal cancer. Alcoholics, like others who are dying, are likely to pass through the phases of denial and isolation, anger, bargaining, and depression. When one gets a clear perspective on alcoholism, the reason for this chilling parallel between progressive alcoholism and other terminal illnesses becomes evident. The fact is: the alcoholic drinks to survive. So long as the mind is insulated by alcohol, a warm and pain-free existence can be maintained. As soon as the alcoholic is deprived of alcohol-on-demand, his or her survival is at stake. It's without the comfort of the bottle that an alcoholic gets a grim and threatening view of life:

—He cannot enjoy life without a sufficient level of alcohol in his bloodstream. The amount varies from little to much. What does not vary is the dependence on the drug. Therefore, to be deprived of alcohol is to be deprived of joy itself.

—The experience induced by alcohol has become a necessary part of her life. Life itself is unacceptable without this experience. Alcohol is an integral element of what she deems the "good life." Therefore, loss of alcohol means loss of what makes life worthwhile.

—Alcohol is the problem-solver in all areas of life. If it is not alcohol, other drugs are required for solutions. Therefore, without a chemical behind which to hide, the alcoholic is overwhelmed by all life's problems.

—The chain reaction—alcohol use, harmful effects, pain, more alcohol for pain relief—produces radical personality changes. An alcoholic can suddenly be swallowed up with selfishness, hostility, and anger. Flights of alcohol-induced fancy seem ridiculous under sober appraisal. Therefore, the alcoholic becomes confused by his own unstable behavior and alarming mood swings.

—As a drinking person, he or she slowly but steadily turns inward, away from social contact (a tightly-packed row of alcoholics is nothing but a series of isolated, lonely people). Removed from reality, the alcoholic's fears are exaggerated. Therefore, drinking induces fear and fear itself becomes a compelling reason to keep drinking.

—An alcoholic's relationship to self, family, employer,

society, and God becomes strained and sometimes broken. Therefore, an alcoholic, especially a *sober* alcoholic, may be sour, bitter, and unappealing to others.

All this the alcoholic realizes as he or she examines life without the blurring of a drug-induced haze. Clarity replaces confusion, pain takes the place of numbness, guilt destroys excuses, alertness drives away sleep, knowledge dispels ignorance, reality is substituted for delusion, and so forth. In reality, all that's happened is that the anesthesia is gone. And that is too much to take. The alcoholic would rather die without pain than live with it. The alcoholic is convinced that without the next drink, the agony of life will become intolerable. Therefore, he or she continues to drink, strengthening the bondage which is, in fact, the source of the agony.

THE SUBCONSCIOUS AND CONFUSION

The forging of an arsenal of denial weapons happens imperceptibly in the lives of most alcoholics. They are sincere in their denial efforts and, sad to say, believe their own defenses are genuine and worth maintaining. With intricate mechanisms of denial assembled deep within the subconscious, the alcoholic seeks to justify himself, protect his own illusion of power, and raise his draining sense of self-esteem. Such ego-building may be practiced in cheap hotels or the loveliest of suburban homes. In either setting, the modern attempt is nothing more than what the Apostle Paul 2,000 years ago called "walking according to the flesh."

But if the denial system has its source in subconscious lies, nevertheless it surfaces with an awesome believability. My own weapons of denial blurred reality effectively while I was convinced I perceived reality flawlessly. White became black, and black, white. The drinking alcoholic doesn't realize he or she lives in an unreal world. It is this effectiveness of denial as a weapon which is so frustrating and infuriating for those nonalcoholic persons who try to help. It is difficult, and often impossible, to communicate effectively with a person living in another world.

But there is more to denial than stubborn willfulness or deliberate deceit. Even when I began soberly reflecting on my own alcoholism, I remained *confused.* I remembered periods of pig-headedness, stubborn resentment, hard-headed selfishness. On the other hand, I remembered periods of intense longing to be free and of sincere attempts to find help. The latter times were suffused with prayers for liberation and renewal. Alcoholism is more than a disease of denial. It is an illness which renders one helpless, hopeless, and especially confused.

People hooked on alcohol do not see what is happening. They cannot find a reason for their anxieties or their moods of self-loathing. Their feelings vacillate between strength and weakness, warm comfort and clammy despair, freedom and bondage.

Contradictory experiences are typical in an alcoholic's life. He does not always drink too much. He may never wrap his car around someone else's radiator although he may have forgotten some morning where he left his auto. He recalls pleasant release and relaxed companionship rather than his bitter words during his most recent drinking episode. Memory blackouts are less frequent than happy remembrances. The interchange of controlled, pleasant drinking and uncontrolled, bad times leads to more and more confusion in the alcoholic's life. Especially in the early stages of alcoholism, he's likely to experience a lack of consistency in drinking patterns. Those slippery places of early addiction are demonic, encouraging the enemy to wield the weapon of denial effectively.

The alcoholic's inability to relate past experiences with present experiences only increases the confusion. As a free Christian, he often gave thanks to God for the wine which made glad the heart of man. He recalls gentle warmth spreading throughout his cold body. He remembers with pleasure his tight muscles relaxing after a tension-filled day. These pleasant experiences were enjoyed by means of a little alcohol "for the stomach's sake." But something happened. Alcohol is no longer the harbinger of pleasure, fun, and relaxation. Now it is frequently accompanied with the pain of excessive or inappropriate behavior. Alcohol intake, once controlled, subtly becomes unmanageable. Mishaps begin to occur. There are memory lapses. Bitter words attack an already eroding self-image. And underneath everything is a gnawing despair which eats away in the pit of the stomach.

These painful current experiences with alcohol are not meaningfully related to the pleasant past events. The alcoholic simply cannot put the past and the present together. What he may once have possessed in joyful moderation now possesses him. Addiction pays him back slowly but surely with the coins of self-reproach, depression, loneliness, confusion, anger, despair, and hopelessness. Events seem unconnected. Sometimes drinking is controlled still, and it seems as if the "good past" is back again. A moment later the "bad present" fills the day. As past and present oscillate in and out of his consciousness, the problem drinker falls victim to his own confusion. And as his confusion increases, his denial mechanisms provide brilliantly deceptive ways of escape. The addicted *Christian* is spared none of the confusion. Indeed, for the Christian, the confusion is merely made the more painful by a piercing sense of guilt.

Often the Christian alcoholic hides his or her deep guilt feelings with a masquerade of piety and health. Most people, after all, have a reservoir of emotions which they do not expose to others. When someone pours a layer of alcohol on top of the reservoir, the result is inevitable confusion. The alcoholic may exude a self-confidence which is no more than a surface of denial painted over a low self-esteem. Just beneath the outgoing big talk is trembling weakness. Below the external appearance of loving concern for others lies naked selfishness. The Christian alcoholic knows Christ "forgets" sins when his brothers and sisters confess their sins, but the alcoholic is plagued with remorse. Regret is written across every part of his life. He feels stained, sordid, unworthy. Although his sins are forgiven by Christ, he cannot forgive himself.

And if such conflicting patterns confuse the alcoholic, they do no less for the alcoholic's family and friends. Feelings of guilt can motivate a frantic striving for perfection; but what a family will see is the struggle to be perfect, not the sense of guilt which motivates it. A poor self-image can show itself in an exaggerated craving for the approval of others, but acquaintances are more likely to see the unseemly drive for approval than the weak self-concept which fuels it. Unless or until an alcoholic's family and friends recognize the illness at work, they may share a common trait with the alcoholic: confusion.

Another fact which adds confusion to the alcoholic's denial is the way he compares himself to others, morally and ethically. This phenomenon is as common today as it was for the Christians in Corinth twenty centuries ago. There were church members who didn't like what the Apostle Paul had taught. They dismissed the teaching by defaming the teacher. Says Paul: "For they say [of me], 'His letters are weighty and strong, but his bodily presence is weak, and his speech of no account.' Let such people understand that what we say by letter when absent, we do when present. Not that we venture to class or compare ourselves to some of those who commend themselves. But when they measure themselves by one another, and compare themselves with one another, they are without understanding" (2 Cor. 10:10-12, RSV). The alcoholic constantly compares himself with others who drink. Watching them, he develops pleasing standards for self-measurement. He discovers that many people drink as much or even more than he does. There are some who regularly introduce their cars to trees and telephone poles, which, of course, he never does. Some drinkers have lost driver's licenses along with marriage licenses, but not he. Other people are Alcoholic—with a capital "A"—but he drinks too much only once in a while. And, after all, all of us are human. We all make mistakes. . . . Looking outside of self for comparison with others, he sees many people with drinking problems worse than his. For him this happy discovery props up all sorts of denial problems.

In the folly of comparing self to others, the alcoholic does not hear—or want to hear—what God says in Proverbs 23:29-35 (RSV):

> *Who has woe? Who has sorrow?*
> *Who has strife? Who has complaining?*
> *Who has wounds without cause?*
> *Who has redness of eyes?*
> *Those who tarry long over wine,*
> *those who go to try mixed wine.*
> *Do not look at wine when it is red,*

when it sparkles in the cup
and goes down smoothly.
At the last it bites like a serpent,
and stings like an adder.
Your eyes will see strange things,
and your mind utter perverse things.
You will be like one who lies down
in the midst of the sea,
like one who lies on the top of a mast.
"They struck me," you will say,
"but I was not hurt;
they beat me, but I did not feel it.
When shall I awake?
I will seek another drink."

While I was still drinking, these words seared me. But much as the passage gnawed at me, I could not stay away from it. Writing sermons, preparing speeches, even fingering through the Bible for evening devotions, I could not stay away from Proverbs 23. God's haunting love would not let me go. And when I stopped comparing myself to others and honestly looked inside myself, the fabric of denial slowly unraveled in a heap of separate, crooked threads. My carefully woven tapestry of denial was shredded, and I began to see my situation with terrible clarity. Confusion was lifted. Finally, under the loving care of God, healing began.

DISARMING DENIAL

After my release from the hospital, a friend confided, "We are co-responsible for your alcoholism." His confession was prompted by a letter he had received criticizing him for cooperating with me in a church-related program. He was told he should have waited until the alcoholic pastor was properly "received back into the fellowship." Apparently the author of that letter banishes alcoholics to the wilderness outside the fellowship of Christ's family.

Such experiences underscore the fact that society in general, and the Christian community in particular, often cannot accept the alcoholic without making demeaning moral and religious judgments. The alcoholic is regarded as weak-willed, immoral, inferior, and above all, ignoble. Think for a moment of words like "drunk," "addict," "boozer," "liquored up," "bombed out," "zonked." Consider their overtones and implications. Watch the next "drunk act" on television. Society denies the *disease* of alcoholism at every turn. Who would laugh at the erratic behaviors of a man with a terminal brain tumor? Who would find his slurred speech and stumbling walk a source of great amusement? By comparison, who has *never* laughed at the drunken character on television or even on the street? The laughable drunk—the funny addict—helps his audience live in comfortable denial of a most uncomfortable truth.

The addict needs denial because he feels in his viscera, at "the gut level," that he is rejected and alone. In spite of well-meant words to the contrary, the alcoholic is isolated from others. He is usually considered weak. Persons close to him constantly urge, "You can quit; just *try* it!" Alcoholics are subtly viewed as immoral, unworthy of the kingdom of God. Such evaluations are communicated to the alcoholic in a barrage of inflections, facial expressions, superior silences, and calculated snubs. These messages get through, loudly and clearly. And as each message is delivered, the alcoholic withdraws a little farther, becomes a bit more confused, and adds another layer of denial.

Through it all, the alcoholic holds on to the one insidious conviction on which denial is founded and by which confusion is retained: "*I can handle it.*" Each word carries its own message:

I: *Self*-worth is kept high.
Can: Power and manageability are mine.
Handle: There are discoverable ways for me to drink
          nonaddictively.
It: This includes alcohol and every other
          mood-altering drug.

The alcoholic works with his or her own special theory which no one can completely disprove. He is convinced, in spite of all his bad experiences, that there is a way to control his drinking. She believes strongly that if she searches long and hard and sincerely, she will be able to manage her use of alcohol. It's a firm conviction which cannot be shaken. And it's understandable. No one enjoys admitting powerlessness. Such admissions do not fit well with society's "macho" concept for men, and our "purity" standards for women. Certainly Christian people believe if they pray often and sincerely, they will have power to do anything not inherently sinful.

Nothing seems to banish this hypothesis of controllable drinking. Bad experiences, visits to the physician (the "scientific priest" for some alcoholics), conferences with employers, counseling with family members, periods of abstinence— nothing removes this essential conviction. The hypothesis of controllability is a persistent, patient enemy of the alcoholic, an enemy dressed in the innocence of self-control. The spark of alcoholism, the hope for controlled drinking, is never extinguished—even after the flame of the disease is quenched.

To keep this spark from bursting into flaming alcoholism again, I am persuaded one needs an action-oriented program like Alcoholics Anonymous. This kind of group interaction keeps the danger of relapse at the level of consciousness. I am thankful to an anonymous friend who once said at a closed AA meeting, "Never, never, *never* forget that we are different. We can't live like others. Our difference is this: We cannot drink alcohol." His intensity of emotion and conviction remains with me. The alcoholic *is* different. He or she *can't* handle alcohol. Others can—we can't! The factual difference is powerlessness and unmanageability. Until that difference is both recognized and admitted, an alcoholic cannot defeat denial or conquer confusion.

Four clusters of events in my life helped disintegrate my own denial system and enabled me to see clearly through my own confusion. Perhaps a personal confession will help others still fettered by denial.

First, there was a painful facing of facts. Gradually, with the help of family and professional counselors, I came to see patterns of drinking which were inappropriate. This awareness was fostered by those who resolutely tried to reduce, rather than heighten, my guilt feelings. Many well-intentioned people, by design, increase the guilt feelings of alcoholics in an effort to help them. I remember having used that tactic myself when dealing with an alcoholic relative. Then I was young. Now I am experienced. I know that to add to the alcoholic's load of guilt will only pressure him or her back into the bottle. To this day, I thank God for sensitive people who helped me see what was happening, who helped remove the guilt which had strapped me for years. Simple facts—not half-truths, tales, innuendos, gossip—dissolve denial. Factual accounts of inappropriateness were presented to me without moral condemnation or religious disapproval. Confrontation, not condemnation, helped me enormously.

Second, there were people (some close to me and others remote from my immediate family) who cared for me as a person. Their basic concern was not for a code of conduct or ecclesiastical opinion or their own image. They risked themselves to reach out to me at a time when I was enslaved, confused, guilty, and hurting. When God finally gave me strength to write openly to my church, one of my sons said, "I don't care if we lose the church and its good opinion. We've got Dad back." That is caring love exercised with clear understanding. Without this kind of concern, I would still be a closet alcoholic.

Third, in attempting to face reality, I educated myself as much as I could on the nature, causes, and consequences of alcoholism. I read every available piece of literature on the subject. As a Christian, I prayed as well as studied. And for hours on end, I talked to other people. The indwelling Christ, using all these means, finally gifted me with the grace of surrender.

While I continue to enjoy sobriety, my esteem for the work of Alcoholics Anonymous, Al-anon, Alateen and similar groups grows. (I could write a separate book about such groups alone.) They have my wholehearted endorsement and grateful thanks.

This brings into focus the fourth factor which helped defeat my denial. It was the experience of group interchange. It is other people with similar problems, failures, hopes, and needs whom God uses to set us on the road of new freedom.

An alcoholic recently cornered me to say, "Alex, Jesus Christ comes to me in other people's lives. I've met Christ in surprising and wonderful ways in all kinds of AA meetings." I too can testify that Christ has met me in the lives of those who, like me, are seeking health. Christ's unexpected and liberating power meets his followers in astounding ways and places.

In summary: (1) factuality, (2) concern and care of others, (3) education, and (4) group interaction were used by the Lord to break down my denial, disarm me, and open the way to acceptance and complete surrender. These factors may be long in forming the impetus for you or someone close to you who denies the disease of alcoholism in his or her life. But never give up on yourself or on someone you love. Christ surprises those who persevere. Even when they ask for no surprises.

FOUR
UNCONDITIONAL
SURRENDER

My son, give me thine heart. Proverbs 23:26, KJV

About a year into my recovery a friend asked if I remembered what I had said to him when he visited me in the hospital. He had found me in the "detox unit" (the hospital ward where an alcoholic is, literally, detoxified, "unpoisoned"). I could vaguely recall that I had poured out my heart to this accepting companion, but I remembered nothing specific.

"I'll never forget it," he said quietly. "You told me, 'I now know what it means to die and rise again.'"

Death cuts all ties. For the alcoholic, unconditional surrender means all strings attached to his or her former drinking patterns must be severed. Both the drinking and the defenses for the drinking need to be buried.

Hospitalization marked my death to an old way of living and a resurrection to a new life. Though I had forgotten my own early confession to a friend, "to die and rise again" is a wonderful five-word description of that experience. Christ's presence became my higher power. His words of invitation, encouraging toward total surrender, took on new and healing power. With inner peace flowing from total release, I turned the whole nightmarish situation over to him. I believed what one of my sons said to me in the treatment center, "Dad, you've got it made now.

Just hang in there and the Lord will put life back together again."

It was not that I refused to accept responsibility for putting myself where I was. On the contrary, I merely recognized that I could no longer try to rescue myself.

ABANDONING SELF

Those who are familiar with the twelve steps of Alcoholics Anonymous know that the first steps teach self-abandonment as the way to self-fulfillment. What they say is:

STEP ONE
We admitted we were powerless over alcohol—that our lives had become unmanageable.

STEP TWO
[We] came to believe that a Power greater than ourselves could restore us to sanity.

STEP THREE
[We] made a decision to turn our will and our lives over to the care of God as we understood Him.

In surrendering, one dies to the old self and its resources. I discovered in my own surrender that, as with other forms of death, this one comes with some pain. My ego was shattered into jagged, disconnected pieces. My self-esteem was covered with guilt, and my guilt seemed unrelated to God's promise of forgiveness. All the gifts of health, family, vocation, material security—none of them brought any contentment. I was flooded with feelings of regret. Perhaps more than at any other time in my life, I appreciated the words of the prophet Jeremiah: "The heart is more devious than any other thing, perverse too; who can pierce its secrets?" (Jer. 17:9, JB)

I knew then that I *wanted* a drug-free life. But I also knew I had no resources left on which to draw. I had laid down my familiar weapons of denial, but had no tools to take up in their place. Even I could no longer deny it: I needed help. I believed it for the first time and believing that, I prayed, "God, help my unbelief!" I had finally died to self as a source, even a partial source, of help toward recovery.

This dying to self involves much more than surrendering to the fact of powerlessness over a drug called alcohol. That part is a *giving up.* The dying also involves *taking up* a full, new life, accepting the "Really Real Self" as needing a total renewal. In the language of Alcoholics Anonymous, surrender means that "steps two through twelve are implied in step one" (see "Twelve Steps of Alcoholics Anonymous," p. 60), much like the petals of a tulip exist in the bulb of the flower.

Fear, guilt, and all the other negatives render one helpless. Help for all broken and impotent lives lies outside humanity in the loving provision of God. Powerlessness to manage and put together the broken pieces of one's "Really Real Self" is the overwhelming experience of a surrendered self. But that does not mean there is no hope, because Jesus announced himself as the fulfillment of these words: "The Spirit of the Lord God is upon me, because the Lord has anointed me to bring good tidings to the afflicted; he has sent me *to bind up the brokenhearted,* to proclaim liberty to the captives, and the opening of the prison to those who are bound . . ." (Isa. 61:18, RSV, author's italics).

The Spirit of Christ provides both a power to shatter old patterns designed for self-destruction and power of sight for new perspectives of life. In a strange and wonderful way the broken are put together, the afflicted hear good news, and the captive are freed.

And the pages of Scripture are covered with praise for genuine brokenness of heart. "The sacrifice acceptable to God is a broken spirit," the psalmist David observes (Ps. 51:17, RSV). "When the righteous cry for help, the Lord hears, and delivers them out of all their troubles. The Lord is near to the brokenhearted, and saves the crushed in spirit" (Ps. 34:17, 18, RSV). In the sterile coolness of a detox unit, I discovered with surprising joy the freedom of a broken heart. The act of breaking apart hurt! Brokenness, however, brought peace. I cried during the breaking and felt calm in the brokenness.

This should not have surprised me. I have in my files a sermon explaining Isaiah 57:15. Rereading that sermon in the past months, I've realized how painfully and blessedly real the prophet's words have become in my life: "For thus says the high and lofty One who inhabits eternity, whose name is Holy: I dwell in a high and holy place, and also with him who is of a contrite and humble spirit, to revive the spirit of the humble, and to revive the heart of the contrite" (RSV).

Surrender means letting go of the illusion that one possesses a hidden supply of power. The experience of brokenness is so overpowering that every remnant of self-defense and denial disappears. Into the momentary vacuum God moves and retrieves broken pieces. He revives the crushed spirit with his presence. The ego, the "Really Real Self," once sinfully fragmented, is refashioned into a fresh pattern of wholeness.

With a sense of profound relief and a sigh of freedom, the newly rescued man or woman exclaims, "Finally, I got myself off my hands!"

GOD'S HANDS

In the hospital I visited the chapel early each morning. I would sit quietly, allowing my thoughts to wander. After a while I would open God's book to listen to him speak to me, usually through the Gospel written by the physician Luke. I was relaxed, open, and attentive, and small packets of God's Word settled into me. Before leaving, I knelt to pray. For the first time in some years, I was speaking to God *confidently,* because I trusted him; *hopefully,* because he had promised release; *calmly,* because I was no longer running. After an active but quiet time, I would go upstairs to the ward to eat with others who also were reaching for some power greater than themselves.

During the early days of rehabilitation, my mind often went to biblical passages on which I had earlier written articles and delivered sermons. Now, with all my thinking being filtered through the experience of recovery, I had new insights into old stories. Fresh meaning colored old truths.

I recalled how King David had proudly ordered a military census. His trust had subtly moved away from God and was centered on his own marching men. God, displeased with David, spoke to him through the prophet Gad and presented the king with three possible punishments: "Shall three years of famine come to you in your land? Or will you flee three months before your foes while they pursue you? Or shall there be three days' pestilence in your land? Now consider, and decide what answer I shall return to him who sent me" (2 Sam. 24:13, RSV).

It was then that David discovered his own powerlessness, and he surrendered himself into the hands of God: "I am in great distress," he cried, "let us fall into the hand of the Lord, for his mercy is great; but let me not fall into the hand of man" (2 Sam. 24:14, RSV). True to his promises, God heard. The plague was averted. Healing spread across the land.

I thought about the Apostle Paul. Stopped on the Damascus road, he asked, "What shall I do, Lord?" Christ told him to wait and listen. Left without sight, food, or drink for three days, Paul waited for Christ to bring him good news. His former self had already been shattered. Now he waited for the reconstructive power which would need to come from beyond himself. And true to his promise, Christ remade "Saul" into "Paul"—not merely a new name, but a new man. In Christ's hand, Paul was made whole.

Sitting by a hospital window, looking into a steady rain, I recalled the Book of Lamentations. God's people had been laid waste; famine ravaged the city of Jerusalem. Women had been reduced to eating their own offspring, the children they once had nursed. Dying husbands were strewn across a nearby battlefield, and in the holy city the house of God had been turned into a mortuary. Death reigned everywhere.

In that pathetic setting the sacred writer urged the people to pour out their deepest feelings. "Arise, cry out in the night, at the beginning of the watches! Pour out your heart like water before the presence of the Lord!" (Lam. 2:19).

When you hold nothing back, then you know what it means to surrender. The poured-out life is a surrendered life. And when life has been surrendered into the hands of God, by the Spirit of Christ, there is a sweeping security—like an infant cradled in the strong arms of his or her father—which turns quiet surrender into a rousing victory.

SURRENDER IS A GIFT

As a Christian, I believe that abandonment, acceptance, surrender, letting go—no matter what word is used—is a *gift*. It is always a gift, even when the gift recipient neither knows nor thanks the Gift Giver.

Once, after I had been out of hospital treatment for some time, I was discussing with another recovering alcoholic the possibility of leaving the pastorate to counsel alcoholics full time. My friend said, "I don't wish to lay anything heavy on you. But I believe that sobriety is a gift of God. And God's gifts are given to share."

My friend's remark about sobriety as "God's gift" sounded strange coming from his lips. He had left the institutional church some years earlier, slamming the door on his way out. He had never shown the slightest interest in religious questions, at least in my presence. After his initial experience of surrender, his sobriety had been interrupted by several lapses into drinking. Finally, he had decided to devote his energies to helping others find a new life of surrender and sobriety; in helping others toward recovery, he had become strong himself. He now heads a firm in a large Midwest city which counsels alcoholics and assists industry with special alcohol and drug programs. He told me that he and his co-workers do not burn out in frustration because they believe that surrender is a free gift of God. While he remains personally related to God, he is sadly estranged from a church community where so many are contentedly ignorant of alcoholism. His sobriety delights me, but his alienation from God's people grieves me.

But for my friend, for me, for all recovering alcoholics, surrender is a gift received in an intensely private manner. Surrender cannot be generated out of the last ounce of strength left in the inner self. It cannot be squeezed out of personal weakness. It originates in the heart of God who heals with strong hands. I cannot count the hours of reading books on alcoholism, the seasons of desperate prayer, the times of hanging on to Bible passages, and the long periods of counseling and discussion which preceded my own day of release on April 19. My Savior and Healer waited long before he gave me this gift. And his gifts, once given, are never taken back. Only within the flow of the surrender experience is this confidence discovered.

ACCORDING TO YOUR WORD

Perhaps the best example of surrender as a gift is found in the life of the blessed mother of our Lord. The angel Gabriel delivered the incredible news of Mary's impending pregnancy: "You will conceive in your womb and bear a son, and you shall call his name Jesus" (Luke 1:31, RSV).

The perplexed virgin was totally powerless. She had never cohabited with Joseph. She knew that her parents would never understand the miracle. The officers and leaders of the synagogue in Nazareth would accuse her of illicit sex. (Joseph, as she soon learned, was no less confused; he didn't know what to do with his young fiancèe either.) Mary had never read anything like Gabriel's story in her Bible, the holy writings. She had nothing comparable in her experience, nothing visible, remembered, or learned to hang on to. All she knew was, "God is with me." And that was enough. She released her life to God who had given her the gift of surrender. "Behold, I am the handmaid of the Lord; let it be to me according to your word" (Luke 1:38, RSV).

God came from beyond every possibility of her life and gave Mary the grace of total self-surrender. She yielded, accepted, believed, let go, free-floated, and allowed her life to be swept along the ways of mystery.

In fact, Mary did three things: she asked for God's help by verbalizing in prayer and asking honest questions; she accepted God's help by meditating on the Lord's ways and by handing over her life for God's use; and she obeyed God's will by deciding to surrender in every way imaginable.

And while Mary was doing these three things, God worked out his plan for her and the whole world: the Holy Spirit prayed for her with sighs too deep for words (Rom. 8:26). The Holy Spirit imparted wisdom and understanding as he overshadowed her. And the Holy Spirit willed and worked his miracle in Mary for the redemption of the world.

The Christian act of surrender is a perfect blend of sovereign divine giving and responsible human decision-making. When God worked this miracle in my life in the special experience of surrender, I never knew when God's work began and mine ended. God's ways *are* above our ways and his thoughts *are* above our thoughts. There is an awesome and wonderful interpenetration of God's actions and the alcoholic's decision to surrender. This makes sobriety an adventure.

CHRIST ELIMINATES THE GAMBLE

Because every act of surrender involves frightening unknowns, one must be ready to take a risk, a gamble. I remember too well my own fear when facing some harsh unknowns. Would I be able to function effectively as a clergyman again if I revealed my personal life with candor? Would members of my congregation be able to overcome whatever bias they had about alcoholism and receive me as someone they could rely on and trust? Would leaders in my denomination's hierarchy block off ways for future service? Would I have enough courage and strength to live openly as a recovering alcoholic? Would I, as an approval-seeking person, be able to handle condemnatory glances, cutting jokes, even honest reports of events I could not remember?

There were no answers to these (and other) questions when I surrendered. I was compelled to walk into the future in simple trust. Life looked like a terrible gamble. It was impossible to live with the cheap retort, "The risk is worth taking because the present and the past are unacceptable." I had been too clever at creative denial to be content with such easy advice. But God removed all fear of the consequences of my risk with his presence. He kept speaking to me about his promises. His presence overshadowed my uncertainty. His steadfast love in Christ disarmed the enemy of fear.

In that time I discovered that surrender was more than mere submission to overwhelming evidence. Yielding to inescapable evidence is basically an exercise of the mind. It functions on an intellectual level. Submission can be nothing more than saying, "I have no choice—I give in."

But surrender is something delightfully different. It is a *decision* to accept God's wisdom, love, power, truth, and mercy. Surrender is pulling the plug on life and allowing all products of ego to go down the drain. Resentment, irritability, pride, despair, anger, and other selfish feelings are flushed away.

One day the *past* was finished. The *future* could be faced tomorrow. The *present* was filled with the strengthening presence of Jesus Christ. Instead of a reluctant submission to power, I experienced a new willingness to yield to the Lord's presence. Acceptance became joyful abandonment. Submission to the evidence was transformed by Christ into eager surrender. The old began to fade as a new day began to dawn.

SELF-IMPROVEMENT WITHOUT CHRIST

Beginning a drug-free life can be likened to sweeping clean your house. Inner resentment, frustration, fear, guilt, hurt, self-depreciation—all the debris can be swept away. It may be possible to reform without acknowledging God's gracious help. It may be possible for life to be put into some kind of order without knowing about supernatural grace. However, improvement of self without claiming and celebrating Christ's renewing strength would have been impossible for me.

The Lord Jesus spoke in a parable about an attempted transformation by self alone: "When the unclean spirit has gone out of a man, he passes through waterless places seeking rest, but he finds none. Then he says, 'I will return to my house from which I came.' And when he comes he finds it empty, swept, and put in order, then he goes and brings with him seven other spirits more evil than himself, and they enter and dwell there; and the last state of that man becomes worse than the first" (Matt. 12:43-45, RSV).

This is as good a picture of a self-improved dry-drunk as can be found. The blood is alcohol-free but inner turmoil remains in suspension. Feelings of jealousy might be temporarily replaced by contentment. Guilt might be driven out by human forgiveness. Anger might be erased with acts of love. Pride might be turned into an honest modesty. Desire for perfection might be postponed. But all such "self-improvements" seldom last. These new patterns of *feelings* eventually disintegrate into chaos. A cleaned-up life needs the permanent presence of the One who will change not only our *feelings* but also our actual *condition*. Christ is the key to the miracle of a surrendered life.

I believe in the need for Christ because I have often read in the

67

gospel accounts, "Go thy way, thy faith has made thee whole."
Jesus gave this promise to a woman plagued by a blood disorder,
to a grateful leper, to a mother pleading for the health of her
child, and to others who needed his power and his presence. It
was the Apostle Paul who, having been met by Christ in a
stunning roadside miracle, later prayed for the Christians in
Ephesus: "that out of his gracious riches he may strengthen you
with power through his Spirit in your inner being, so that Christ
may dwell in your hearts through faith. And I pray that you,
being rooted and established in love, may have power, together
with all the saints, to grasp how wide and long and high and deep
is the love of Christ, and to know this love that surpasses
knowledge—that you may be filled to the measure of all the
fullness of God" (Eph. 3:16-19, NIV).

It must be clearly understood that Christ graciously enters the
sinner's life by way of faith. This way is not to be confused with
the cheap "believism" so often touted in the mass media in North
America. One does not "just accept Jesus" or "just believe he
died for you." One's response cannot be a dull "I guess so" or
"maybe it will happen" or "I hope he'll come to me." No! Faith is
the root from which grows the fruit of power, joy, peace,
gentleness, joy, self-control and all other Christian graces. Faith
plants one's personal existence into the soil of Christ's presence.
In him, the redeemed continue to bring forth big harvests at the
right time. And this faith, like surrender, is a *gift*. It is provided
by God's Spirit, not manufactured out of one's inner resources;
therefore, one asks for faith as one requests a gift—cautiously,
humbly, knowing there is no bargain or payment one can make.
When faith is given, it is accepted with thanks, and gratitude
marks the everyday lives of those who receive this unparalleled
gift.

I think of faith as a total commitment which engrafts me into
Christ and makes me whole. When God gives this gift, he makes
us able to:

1. *Relate to Jesus as a person.* We read the Gospels, watch him
work the Father's will, and feel his presence. He acts today in his
personal word and spiritual presence, and we can meet him hour
by hour.

2. *Be open to his presence.* We refuse to shut out his energy, truth, wisdom, love, and other perfections by preconceived ideas which are set in the concrete of our limited experience. He may, he *does*, surprise us.

3. *Receive gifts from God.* We can receive gifts like Simon Peter received the revelation of Christ. "Flesh and blood did not reveal" the messianic secret of Jesus to that fisherman. It was Christ's Father in heaven who gave the gift of insight. He still gives that gift today.

4. *Tap into God's power.* We know in the depths of our being the power which raised Christ from the dead and let him sit on the right hand of power. We can feel the Lord powerfully working. We know that through Christ, we can do all things.

5. *Wager our lives on God without risk.* We stake everything on the One who went through death and hell. He came out alive! He is our companion, our older brother, who really knows, accepts, and loves us. He sticks with you and me through every experience, even through the end called *death* which he turns into victory.

6. *Be mastered by the truth.* We are absolutely persuaded that God's diagnosis of our predicaments is true. His provisions of salvation fit our concrete experiences exactly.

7. *Pledge loyalty to a friend who never breaks his word.* With the handshake of early morning loyalty, the real believer walks in newness of life with the One who never lets him go. My empty hand is grasped by his outstretched hand, which is full of unexpected gifts everyday.

8. *Abide in him every day.* When he left our earth from Mt. Olivet, he said, "Lo, I am with you always, even to the end of the age." Christ and the Christian are joined eternally.

Everyone describes his personal experience of faith in a special, one-of-a-kind way. Every person is unique, special to God, and important to Christ. Christ enters and dwells in the house of our lives today as genuinely as he visited Zaccheus in Jericho two centuries ago. Believe it or not, he wants to surprise every man and every woman with his permanent presence. Faith is the road he takes to arrive in our lives as a permanent companion.

And all of this is no less true for the alcoholic than for any other human being.

STRENGTH IN UNION

Surrender is the key to a new life because when I surrender, Christ and my "Really Real Self" are fused, are united, become one. In that union is the source of permanent health for all who suffer the illness of alcoholism.

Between Christ and every Christian is a *spiritual* union. The Christian's "higher power" is not some physical power derived from electrons or protons. Neither is it some moral power which joins Christ's (good) will with mine. Rather, there are two lives joined together by the Holy Spirit in the kind of oneness in which neither Christ nor the Christian loses his or her identity. In the Spirit, the Christian "knows," "feels," and "senses" that he or she no longer lives but "Christ Jesus lives in" him.

Admittedly, the union is *mystical.* The oneness between Christ and his brothers and sisters is not irrational, but neither can it be exhaustively described in terms of feelings, affections, or volitions. It is a oneness which escapes precise analysis. Just when the Christian tiptoes near to see this mystical reality, he stops to worship in the presence of the light so iridescent, a beauty so sensitive, that he joins an aging King David in childlike wonder: "I am not concerned with great affairs or marvels beyond my scope. Enough for me to keep my soul tranquil and quiet, like a child in its mother's arms, as content as a child that has been weaned" (Ps. 131:1, 2, JB).

And this union is a *life* union. As a branch in the vine, the Christian's life bears fruit. From Christ, who is my life, comes a surge of the Spirit's vitality which brings forth the fruit of love, joy, peace, patience, kindness, goodness, fidelity, gentleness, and self-control (see Galatians 5). And every branch that bears fruit, he trims clean so it will bear more fruit (see John 15).

Finally, this union is *indissoluble.* No one can snatch the Christian out of Christ's hand. Christ completes the work of healing he begins. He tells the Christian not to be troubled. Future glory is the perfection of his promise, and his promise is sufficient.

CHRIST BRINGS MEANING

I have been writing as a Christian, describing what Christians have long believed. But all these teachings have very special meaning to me not simply as a Christian but especially as a Christian recovering alcoholic.

By accepting the truth of my union with Christ, I know now that I am never alone, even during times of isolation, loneliness, and fear. Even when I was in bondage to alcohol, he was with me. He never left even though he had every reason to abandon me. He understood the painful ambivalence of a life abound, yet free. He knows my frailty and always tenderly remembers that I am dust.

And for today, he is present to give life. In those desperate moments when suicide seemed the easy, simple, single answer, I see now that it was he who invited, summoned, remonstrated, coaxed, prayed, and kept talking to me. The depths of lost self-esteem were not too low for him. He remained present with promises of hope, love, and healing. And he will remain tomorrow as well.

It was his presence that brought healing into view and he always made it available in his invitations. Through many of his followers, members of his body, he kept the ways to freedom and health wide open. His prescriptions for a new life were not easy. His advice was never cheap. His love was sometimes stern. But his insistence that I change never came with sullen impatience or condemnatory condescension. No matter where he directed my wounded life, he went along to strengthen and encourage.

In the raw pain of my persistent loneliness, in the dark hours of my unbelief, he was always present. He took away my sordidness, failure, guilt, pride, and everything else which disfigured my life. He showed me the bruises he suffered for my transgressions. In his presence I could see the stripes by which I was healed. And when I needed a word of comfort or hope or instruction, he was there to speak emphatically, directly, personally, and effectively.

All this and much more are wrapped up in this special experience of "Christ in me, the hope of glory." And, believe it or not, he says to everyone—including the most clever drunk—"Whoever comes unto me I will in no wise cast out!"

His coming does not necessarily mean tenderness, gentleness.

God can be wind and fire. His words can hit like a hammer. He gives strength, but often only after he has shown us our glaring weaknesses. He helps in ways we don't want or expect.

Sometimes he shatters our illusions: particularly, the lie that drugs like alcohol improve things. Sometimes he allows us to endure terrifying darkness before experiencing the warm light of new perceptions. He brings his sons and daughters to glory. The road may be long, hard, even dark. But his presence makes the journey possible and the goal meaningful.

FIVE
IN TOUCH
WITH SELF

I do not understand my own actions. For I do not do what I want, but I do the very thing I hate. Romans 7:15, RSV

The problem of the alcoholic is not alcohol. It is himself or herself. The recovering alcoholic has painfully clear insight into the old saying, "I am my own worst enemy."

The journey into freedom from drugs requires that the surrendered person find a way to be "in touch with self." It is not meant to be a self-centered way of life; rather, it is a search for the self (the "Really Real Self") which requires both courage and time. After all, many of us do not know who we really are, and nearly everyone suffers an identity crisis at one time or another. For one whose identity has been drawn from a bottle, the turning away from alcohol is the first move in a search for a new identity, a new "self." To state it simply: the recovering alcoholic needs more than a new image—he or she needs a new identity, needs to become a "new person." Finding that new self is both critical and traumatic.

It is at this point that steps four through seven of the Alcoholics Anonymous program can best be introduced:

STEP FOUR
[We] made a searching and fearless moral inventory of ourselves.

STEP FIVE
[We] admitted to God, to ourselves, and to another human being the exact nature of our wrongs.

STEP SIX
[We] were entirely ready to have God remove all these defects of character.

STEP SEVEN
[We] humbly asked Him to remove our shortcomings.

A BIBLICAL PERSPECTIVE ON SELF

In the Old Testament we read the story of Prime Minister Hazael who did not know himself (2 Kings 8). Seeing tears in the eyes of Elisha the prophet, he asked, "Why does my Lord weep?" The prophet responded by telling Hazael about the evil the prime minister would one day commit: ". . . you will slay [Israel's] young men with the sword, and dash in pieces their little ones, and rip up their women with child." Indignant, Hazael exclaimed, "What is your servant, who is but a dog, that he should do this great thing?" But after Hazael had murdered King Benhadad, he went on to wield power with ruthless hatred and violence. He had apparently not known his own latent, and potent, evil.

The alcoholic has a hard time, too, honestly facing the complexities and conflicts of his or her inner self. The good he wants to perform, he fails to do. The evil that she does not want to do, she does. Because he or she wants to keep in constant touch with the inner self, the Christian alcoholic soon learns to adopt the prayer of David: "God, examine me and know my heart, probe me and know my thoughts; make sure I do not follow pernicious ways, and guide me in the way that is everlasting" (Ps. 139:23, 24, JB).

In the New Testament we hear Saul, transformed into Paul, looking back on his "self" and describing himself with words like "flesh," "sin," "slavery," "conflict," and so forth. "But I am carnal, sold under sin," he laments in one place (Rom. 7:14, RSV).

The concept of carnality ("flesh") implies all that is common to crippled human nature since that awful fall in the Garden. We can distinguish at least three powerful forces which emerge from our carnality, our "flesh."

The first is the power of *imperialism*. The power-hungry self wants to stake out more territory to conquer. It seeks more people to manipulate. It wants to act like God in arranging the affairs of others to suit its own purposes. And it is adamantly opposed to the character of divine love which molds Christ's brothers and sisters, a love which never seeks its own ends (1 Cor. 13:5).

The second is the power of *impatience*. The carnal self wants immediate gratification of all its desires and needs. The carnal person does not know what it means to wait upon the Lord because he or she cannot wait for anyone or for anything. This power is at war in the Christian with that love which is always patient (1 Cor. 13:4, 7).

Then, third, there is the power of *intolerance*. It is the power of the all-knowing self. The carnal self spits out cutting, bitter words to push aside differing opinions. Such intolerance often inflicts wounds in others by shunting aside the self-sacrificing love Paul describes in 1 Corinthians 13 and by assuming a self-building power over other people and their lives.

Both in and above one's fleshly tendencies is sin. Many people are willing to accept the idea of "sin" as a primitive term to describe what goes wrong in the world. But the Bible insists that sin is more than a general sense of mankind's mistaken attitudes and behaviors. Sin is part of what people *are;* it is within us, and infects our selves as a cancer infects (and thereby becomes a part of) a cell. The Bible personifies sin (in the words of Paul). It springs to life, deceives, revives after being asleep, and even kills.

And, in the biblical perspective, "flesh" is the weak spot in the self which sin seeks out and invades. It is purely personal in detail. My weak "flesh" spots may be different from yours; my strong point may be your weak point, and vice versa. But whatever the detailed patterns carnal living may eventually take, Paul's description (Rom. 7:15-17, 20, RSV) of the battle against sin remains incisively true: "I do not understand my own actions. For I do not do what I want, but I do the very thing I hate. Now if

I do what I do not want, I agree that the law is good. So then it is no longer I that do it, but sin which dwells within me."

In Paul's words, one senses a crisis of identity—confusion. Although it is a difficult task, everyone who wants to live free from drugs *must* reach to his or her real, deep-down self. Why? Because it is this self, with all its contradictions, which has been accepted by Christ as it is.

It is in knowing that Christ has taken charge that the sinner can feel comfortable with him- or herself. That is not a self-satisfied sort of comfort, but a self-accepting sense of belonging. The self-image and the self finally fit together with ease. If Christ could value one's carnal self enough to love that self and by his Spirit to dwell within that self, then we too can accept our selves without the euphoria produced by a drug. In Christ's presence every person can be completely honest with himself and herself. It is no longer necessary—it is no longer possible!—to put up a phony front.

DEALING WITH FEELINGS

Many people, especially Christian people, ignore their feelings. For years I alternately fought bad feelings because they were painful and opposed good feelings because they seemed too pleasurable to be God-pleasing. Feelings had become enemies to be defeated, pests to be banished, pressures to be suppressed. Today I am grateful to counselors who helped me live with my feelings (both good and bad). A thorough analysis of feelings would demand more discussion than I can provide here, but at least four feelings plague most alcoholics and these need to be addressed.

RESENTMENT. Common to most drug-dependent people is the feeling of *resentment.* Take the word apart: "re" means "again" and "sentare" means "to feel." Resentment is a re-feeling of all the irritations, unjust criticisms, and unfair hurts (real or imagined) that tarnish life. Those feelings become the seeds which, when cultivated by pride, reap a bitter harvest of resentments.

In order to handle resentments, a person needs to become

mature. Many adults act like spoiled children whose inflated egos nurse feelings of self-pity. For an alcoholic, those feelings are turned into a justification for continued drinking. To be liberated, one needs to learn how to put resentment aside. What are the lessons that must be learned? At least these six:

First, it is imperative to accept one's place in God's scheme of things. The world is his, not ours. We must accept ourselves as having *a* place, not *the* place of prominence, in his plan for his creation. The virtue we need is true humility. Without it we are resentful not only of other people but also of our Maker.

Second, one must accept others as he or she learns to accept self—with all the human limitations and faults intact. A person maimed by resentments is waiting for the approval of others in order to bolster self-esteem. In setting aside such resentments, we also set aside the temptation to approve of others only when they have proven themselves perfect, blameless, or more-than-human.

Third, one must develop a sense of humor as protection from the searing brushfires of resentment. Humor helps keep life's irritations in balance. By learning to smile at painful episodes in life, one renders such events impotent as resentment-builders.

Fourth, one needs to cultivate simple pleasures and savor the delightful, but commonplace, events in life. There are more little pleasures than big thrills. Enjoy the smell of rain on a hot sidewalk, the bird's song, the rose's sweet scent, and a walk in the woods. There is no room for resentment in a life filled with simple joys.

Fifth, live neither in the past nor in the future, but enjoy the present. The past *is* past. And the future is not here. Remember yesterday, plan for tomorrow, and enjoy this day the Lord has given.

And sixth, the person struggling with resentment must learn to welcome work. It is a most basic, created function for human beings. As soon as God made Adam and Eve, he put them to work. The satisfaction of accomplishment is a balm which cures the inevitable hurts of life.

ANGER. A first cousin to resentment is *anger.* When we experience the emotion of anger, we are annoyed, irritated, and upset; we become furious. Anger is often the raw energy of emotion in response to a hurt, a loss, a disappointment, a betrayal—any intensely painful experience. Sometimes it is directed at a person or object perceived as "the enemy." An alcoholic often discovers that "the enemy is me."

We tend to lock anger inside ourselves along with those other feelings which cause damage. One likes to think of him- or herself as in control. Pride, our love affair with self, demands that we never let ourselves go, never let loose the controls of our life. Besides, to show anger is to risk the disapproval of others; angry people are not acceptable and lovable.

We cannot deal with anger if we suppress it. It merely pops out in other forms—headaches, backaches, ulcers, constipation, alcoholism, physical abuse, or other forms of violence.

For the Christian, especially the Christian alcoholic, the means by which anger can be controlled is found in Christ. He who was crucified by an angry mob is able to supply the mature courage which conquers our rising angers. To handle anger appropriately, one must remember that he or she is not allowed to play God. Christ is the judge of all people and all events. Where judgments are needed, he will provide them. Our calling is to stay close to Christ, and let him judge.

In Christ's presence one can acknowledge anger without being swept away by it. Christ enables us to perform an act of love, allowing it to take the place of our desire for revenge. As he did at Calvary, so in our lives, Christ can transform energy for evil into power for good.

GUILT. Guilt plagues all people, but especially the alcoholic. Angry people who bury feelings in a windowless soul are those who suffer the sharpest pain of guilt.

Guilt is the feeling of blameworthiness. It threatens a person with all kinds of punishment, real and imagined. He experiences an oppressive, gnawing apprehension deep down in the viscera; she feels completely vulnerable to rejection, isolation, imprisonment, and even hell.

It is essential to distinguish between authentic guilt and imagined guilt. Think of this example: If I smash my neighbor's back door window and rob her house, I should incur *real* guilt.

The next night I may repent, fix the window, and replace the stolen jewelry and cash. This act of restitution does not, however, remove my guilt. The law was broken. My liability remains even though I have repaired the physical damage and replaced the material loss. Real, authentic guilt is objective. It is more than a feeling. It is a broken relationship which only a judge can repair in a court of law.

Imaginary guilts are subjective feelings. They have no adequate basis in experienced reality, no validity in a court of law. But these false guilts are ghastly for the person who is plagued by them. They drain his or her energy and can effectively destroy happiness and well-being.

In the presence of both the fact and the feeling of guilt, there is this good news: Jesus came not to condemn but to save. His perfect work on earth totally removes all the authentic guilt of believers. Jesus was incensed with the religious leaders of his day who ignored genuine guilt while inducing imagined guilt. "You load men with burdens hard to bear," he told them, "and you yourselves do not touch the burdens with one of your fingers" (Luke 11:46, RSV). God is eager to forgive and remove the burdens of guilt from one's life. "Come now, let us reason together," is the message he delivers to us; "though your sins are like scarlet, they shall be as white as snow; though they are red like crimson, they shall become like wool" (Isa. 1:18, RSV).

FEAR. In addition to resentment, anger, and guilt is *fear.* Fear is the emotion most keenly felt right after an alcoholic shuts off drug intake. The alcoholic is afraid that he or she will not be able to live life without the daily painkiller. The pain of the fearful person ranges all the way from mild apprehension to sheer panic. Between those two extremes, one feels jittery, nauseated, clammy, and shaky. Every one of us lives in a threatening world. Besides the threats common to humanity, the alcoholic is daily threatened by that innocent-appearing, attractively advertised beverage.

Fear often focuses on the threat of loss. One fears the loss of personal life in death or one may be afraid of losing a loved one. This person dreads losing her job. That one fears the loss of his self-esteem. One fears inflation, fire, cancer, and the unknown.

Fearful people are often unduly concerned about losing the approval of others. And we all may, to one extent or another, exaggerate the grounds for our fears, allowing our fears to grow far out of proportion to the real possibility of harm.

It is necessary to see the objects of one's fear for what they are. It is *not* necessary or helpful, in an attempt to preserve a "macho" image, to become a phony and say, "I don't care what you think of me" or "I don't care what happens to me." Rather, one must define and face fear openly, courageously, and honestly.

To conquer some fears, one must cultivate the art of letting go. Paul's words, rightly understood and urgently prayed over, may help one overcome the fear of loss. He wrote: "Brothers, this is what I mean: our time is growing short. Those who have wives should live as though they had none, and those who mourn should live as though they had nothing to mourn for; those who are enjoying life should live as though there were nothing to laugh about; those whose life is buying things should live as though they had nothing of their own; and those who have to deal with the world should not become engrossed in it. I say this because the world as we know it is passing away" (1 Cor. 7:29-31, JB).

The Lord's presence helps track down a specific fear to its earliest perceived appearance. Frequently, if one is able to locate the origin of his or her fear, the fear itself quickly begins to shrink to the size it actually deserves. It is foolish to underestimate or exaggerate our fears. Christ, our wisdom, gives us insight to track down our fears, helping us determine what we are genuinely afraid of losing.

TAKING YOUR INVENTORY

In my religious tradition each believer is expected to engage in a thorough self-examination before eating and drinking the elements in Holy Communion. In the continuing program of recovery from alcoholism, it is imperative to take a rigorous personal inventory in order to continue an alcohol-free and drug-free life.

The "Big Book" of Alcoholics Anonymous has this to say about self-inventory:

We believe the acts of drunkenness, dishonesty, envy, self-pity, spite, hatred, resentment, malice, and injustice not only injure us, but are the acts of depraved people in the eyes of society and opposed to all spiritual virtues known to AA members who have been spiritually awakened. If these be spiritual debits, then most of us have drunk ourselves into spiritual bankruptcy. Notwithstanding the great necessity of discussing ourselves with someone, it may be one is so situated that there is no suitable person available. If that is so, this step may be postponed only, however, if we hold in complete readiness to go through with it at the first opportunity. We say this because we are very anxious that we talk to the right person. It is important that he be able to keep a confidence; that he fully understands and approves what we are driving at; that he will not try to change our plan. But we must not use this as a mere excuse to postpone. When we have decided who is to hear our story, we waste no time. We pocket our pride and go to it, illuminating every twist of character, every dark cranny of the past. . . . Once we have taken this step, we are delighted. We can look the world in the eye. We begin to feel the nearness of our Creator. We have had certain spiritual beliefs, but now we begin to have a spiritual experience.

Several resources are available. One, related to self-inventory, is so helpful it deserves special mention: "The Guide to Fourth Step Inventory" (obtainable from Hazelden, Box 11, Center City, Minnesota, USA, 55012) is a detailed and clearly written aid to any recovering alcoholic. This guide helps tremendously by encouraging a fearless honesty, openness with understanding others, and day-by-day effort in ongoing recovery.

Taking a personal inventory takes time. But done patiently and persistently, the effort benefits one in various ways. A person gets to know him- or herself better and comes to accept the authentic self with Christian ease rather than superficial complacency. One sees the need for specific, daily change when regularly taking a self-inventory (especially if done with other recovering alcoholics). Danger signals which place sobriety into jeopardy are likely to be spotted during such inventories. This recognition, often very special and private, keeps one away from the "first drink." By looking closely at ourselves, we learn to be more patient in living with others who also suffer defects and shortcomings. And in all self-inventory, the presence of Christ becomes the power which enables a recovering alcoholic to move from strength to strength.

What helped me as an outpatient at the hospital was the use of the materials which were compiled by Dr. Donald A. Tubesing. Copies of this material were obtained from the Wholistic Health Center, 30 E. Fourth Street, Hinsdale, Illinois 60521. Try keeping the following statements in mind as you use this tool to keep in touch with yourself. These statements, although influenced by Dr. Tubesing, are mine, and are not the responsibility of Dr. Tubesing.

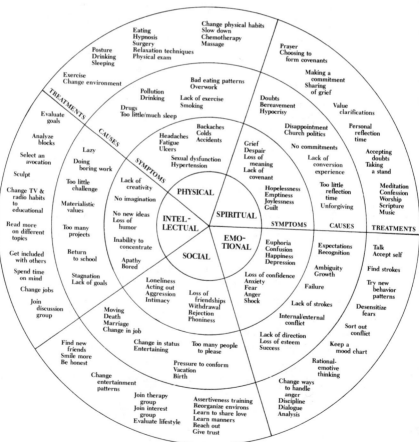

Alcoholism can be graphically represented as a wheel containing a hub surrounded by three concentric circles. The hub contains the words *physical, emotional, intellectual, social,* and *spiritual.* The concentric circles present symptoms, causes, and treatment. The way alcoholism shows itself in each person's life is unique. In some lives the spiritual and emotional aspects predominate. It was so in my life. But remember this, regardless of differences in detailed manifestation, there is a similarity of experience common to all alcoholics. Personally, my religious selfhood described in chapter 3, my relationship to Jesus Christ, gave breadth of perspective and depth of understanding to my experience of alcoholism.

Focus first on the symptoms listed in each sector of the diagram which begins at the hub of the wheel and expands towards the circumference. This exercise must be repeated, perhaps every day at first. You may not think you possess a certain symptom. The more honestly you look at yourself and your life, the more symptoms you discover. At least this happened to me.

Examine the *causes* of these symptoms with the same patience and persistence as you examined the symptoms. No doubt you will uncover personal causes not listed in the diagram.

The treatment needed, desired, and available should be studied with the help of others. You can explore the sections on symptoms and causes with others who are close to you. In fact, this is highly recommended. Symptoms and causes are more private than treatments. Be sure to speak with others, especially those who are knowledgeable about alcohol and drug abuse. When I did this, I found more treatment resources available to me than I had ever dreamed existed. Christ used many of these resources to bring healing into my life.

SIX
IN TOUCH
WITH OTHERS

As iron sharpens iron, so man sharpens his fellowman. Proverbs 27:17, NASB

The first person *plural* pronoun—we—is a very important word. In our time of so much narcissism (obsessive self-love), when "I do my thing" is the *in* thing, it is instructive to note that the singular personal pronouns "I" and "me" are not used even once in the twelve steps of Alcoholics Anonymous. "We," "our," and "us" are used. (Christians have often observed the same thing in the perfect prayer—the "Our Father"—taught by Christ Jesus.)

It is no wonder that recovering alcoholics who continue to enjoy victory meet together. Alcoholics form groups because recovery from their disease is remarkably successful when shared with others. All "I'll-do-it-myself" programs fail. Such efforts are doomed to failure because one needs the insight of others to discover one's true self. In group interaction, alcoholics help each other open up to disclose problems which have been bottled up for a long time. Others assist in identifying the roadblocks we use to shut out our own feelings.

Self-delusion is common. One of the things about which we easily delude ourselves is the delusion itself—that is, we delude ourselves into thinking we aren't deluded. One of the most helpful devices used in therapy to help me see my own self-delusions was the "Johari Window." It is a "window" with four labeled panes, usually drawn like this:

SELF

	OPEN (1)	CLOSED (2)
O T H E R S	BLIND (3)	UNCONSCIOUS (4)

The four windowpanes represent four aspects of the total self. As the diagram indicates, only the top two panes (1 and 2) are visible to me (the "self"). The two panes on the left-hand side (1 and 3) are visible only to others. The lower right-hand pane (4, unconscious) is usually invisible both to me and to others.

Windowpane one is labeled "open." This part of life is visible to me and to others. It contains the material I am willing to share with others: my interests, vocation, family, abilities, and so forth.

Windowpane two contains the word "closed." This part of life refers to the secrets about the self which one does not wish to show to others. One fears the loss of esteem if others see feelings of hostility, suspicion, inferiority, pride, greed, jealousy, resentment, or self-pity. Such feelings are sealed in (or "closed").

Windowpane three contains the word "blind." One is blind to self, but not to others. The tone of voice, tilt of the head, shifting of eyes, deep sighs, trembling hands—all reveal things about the self to which a person is often blind. Many times a counselor can see more in a counselee in one-half hour than a person can see in him- or herself during years of self-examination. The material behind pane three may be evident to others, but I am "blind" to it.

Windowpane four represents the unconscious. It is invisible. While various techniques may help one penetrate the unconscious, this penetration is a by-product and not a goal of group interaction. Recognizing the unconscious source of many feelings is not essential to recovery from alcoholism; what is necessary is that we accept our feelings and learn to cope with them.

CONFRONTATION

When someone tells another person how he or she appears—what an observer sees in pane three—there is *confrontation*. Confrontation is essential for continuing recovery.

Confrontation can be defined as presenting a person with an image of himself or herself by describing how one sees him or her. Confrontation is helpful only when spoken with concern. It must be accompanied with specific data; for example:

> You seem self-centered to me because, whenever we talk, you want to talk only about yourself.
>
> I know you believe you're in mourning. But frankly, having listened to you over the past months and wanting to help, I think you are feeling sorry for yourself. I think you're hooked on self-pity.

To confront is to describe what one has observed in the person being confronted. Guesses, advice, or discussion about things we witness are not confrontations. Confrontation is like holding up a mirror to let another person know how he or she *appears* to others. While it may sometimes be painful, it can also be the kindest courtesy. It allows a person to correct what may, in fact, be *mis*impressions caused *only* by appearances. Or it may help a person come to grips with what he or she actually does feel but wants to deny to self. Confrontation often needs to take place before a person will seek healing alone or in a group. Family, employers, and others who live close to alcoholics can use confrontation to motivate the sick person to seek help. And, once motivated and in treatment, it enables a person to have "group therapy" which is actually self-therapy in a group.

One is most helpful as confronter when he or she refuses to try to change the other person and only desires to help another see him- or herself more accurately. Change will come *at its own pace* and *in its own time*. And some alcoholics—as with many nonalcoholics—will tragically die before they change, even though they have been strongly and lovingly confronted. But confrontation does not mean that we accept responsibility for another person's behavior or feelings. It merely means we describe to another what we see, and we describe our observations as accurately and fairly as possible.

Because of blindness which feeds self-delusion, every person remains dependent on others for a complete picture of self. Confrontation is an essential tool for building the entire picture.

LEVELING

To respond openly when confronted is to "level." (Think of the saying, "Let me level with you.") One levels when one takes the risk of being known by openly unveiling one's feelings. Leveling is a vital part of recovery for alcoholics.

Bottled-up anger and hidden fear will lead to more relapses than most other feelings. And anger and fear, along with anxiety, are usually the hardest feelings to report. In a typical group therapy session, a recovering alcoholic is taught to name his or her feelings; simply giving names to feelings is an important act in itself. Until one can accurately identify (name) what one feels, it is usually impossible to deal with the feeling until it is out of control.

If one responds in a group meeting *without* naming a feeling, that person is said to be "hiding behind defenses." Examples of the defenses, walls behind which people hide feelings, include: explaining, justifying, silence, attacking, humor, long pauses to analyze, simply agreeing or disagreeing (without accepting responsibility). Each defense serves to avoid naming the feelings one is experiencing and taking responsibility for dealing with the feeling.

For the most part, defenses are unconscious, automatic shields against a real or imagined threat to self-esteem. By pointing out the defenses a person uses, one can help this person eliminate the barrier which is locking others out as well as getting closer to ourselves. Coming to recognize these blocks to self-discovery may enable us to look behind them where we can discover the feelings concealed from view. Since defenses hide us not only from others but also from ourselves, it is important to identify them consciously, that is, not only saying (in words) what the feeling is but also accepting the fact that those words are accurate and true.

In many areas of life, a sense of modesty is appealing. That's also true when dealing with our own feelings. It isn't necessary or even noble for people to be so loose with their emotions that they are constantly flaunting how they feel about themselves or others. But alcoholics tend to err in the opposite direction, and so do many others. We tend to think we already know ourselves, but it is hard to take the risk of being revealing and genuine. We are, quite simply, frightened of our own emotions.

In similar moments, when you are tempted to withdraw into silence or cover up your feelings, remember that every person knows fear. Remember too that the indwelling Christ knows, understands, forgives, and gives courage.

To the person who drowns negative feelings in alcohol, I would urge: Try leveling with your feelings of fear and anger. Discover how good—even in the face of fear—leveling can make you feel. Bad feelings can lose a great deal of power when recognized, and we can gain strength when revealing them to others. As leveling and confronting take place with others, we discover that we can identify not only anger and fear, but also a whole array of feelings: anxiety, resentment, concern, defiance, smugness, self-pity, worthlessness, hostility, empathy, rejection, superiority, evasiveness, despair, acceptance, sympathy, arrogance, inadequacy, defensiveness, and so on.

Most people have ignored or denied these feelings for years. Christ, the Searcher of our inner selves, can lead us to new openness, freedom, and peace. In truth, he offers us a whole new life—also with regard to our own feelings.

RECOVERING RELATIONSHIPS

As a recovering alcoholic learns to handle personal feelings, he or she is enabled to live more comfortably with other people, many who may have been hurt while the drinking continued. The most painful moment in my own recovery was when I came to grips not only with what I had done to myself, but especially with how my illness had violated people nearest to me. At this point, members of Alcoholics Anonymous move into the eighth, ninth, and tenth steps on the road to recovery.

STEP EIGHT
[We] made a list of all the persons we have harmed, and
became willing to make amends to them all.

The key word in step eight is "willing." Openness to one's
inner self enables a new openness with others. The alcoholic,
while still drinking, broods in resentment and loneliness. The
recovering alcoholic wants to leave the gray, angry world of
loneliness. Like any healthy person, he or she eagerly desires to
heal sick relationships and rebuild broken friendships. AA
meetings, group therapy sessions, easy conversations with
counselors—all are used by Christ Jesus to help us discover new
ways to love and live.

Love is rooted in the will ("become willing"), and it is a
steady direction of the will to seek the good of the other ("make
amends to them all"). Once one decides to care enough to make
a precise list of persons who were hurt, it becomes possible to go
to such persons and say, "I'm sorry for what I did and said. I was
so wrong! Will you forgive me?"

An honest, ready willingness to live this way is an exciting step
along the road of victory.

STEP NINE
[We] made direct amends to such people wherever
possible, except when to do so would injure them or others.

A willingness to make amends means one jettisons every form
of pride, begins to think first of the person or persons harmed,
and seeks to discover what is best for them. Willingness to make
amends in love involves walking in the other person's shoes or
sitting in the other person's chair. To pour balm into the wounds
with love's unique desire may mean *not* saying anything
immediately because someone you hurt is not yet ready to be
restored. Step nine requires that we seek reconciliation on the
other person's terms and timeline, for his or her good, avoiding
all new injury.

Some of the best advice I received while in treatment was
given in the words every recovering alcoholic must learn to
practice: "Take it easy. . . . Easy does it." Slowly one learns to

leave the self-destructive pattern of hurrying to another place, another relationship, another refuge, another drink.

Impatience is not easily overcome, especially when you want to try repairing in a single day what you broke over a period of years, to heal in an instant what you poisoned over a lifetime. There are no quick fixes for the hurts of other persons. And those for whom we have the deepest love may also have suffered the deepest hurts. Tender concern for others must color one's eagerness to make amends, and love must be allowed to heal with patience. At this point one asks the indwelling Christ to work. With him in control, victory is assured.

STEP TEN
[We] continued to take personal inventory and when we were wrong, promptly admitted it.

Alcoholics are never allowed the luxury of forgetting their sickness. It is their responsibility to keep the level of personal alertness high and sharp. In the lazy glow of forgetfulness, one can become convinced that "it's all behind me now" and reach out for that "first drink" again. Thanks to the indwelling Christ I have not forgotten how frail my strength is and how fragile my freedom is.

It is easy to listen but difficult to act when it comes to personal inventory. Step ten keeps the heart alert and the will poised to daily decision. I'm glad for the words from the New Testament letter signed by James. He spoke of self-deception in these words: "For if any one is a hearer of the word and not a doer, he is like a man who observes his natural face in a mirror; for he observes himself and goes away and at once forgets what he was like. But he who looks into the perfect law, the law of liberty, and perseveres, being no hearer that forgets but a doer that acts, he shall be blessed in his doing" (James 1:23-25, RSV). The doer promptly admits his wrong.

For the alcoholic, many a drink is poured and swallowed because it seems like the easiest way to answer life's questions. During recovery, the compulsive drinker learns to face life's sorriest moments—when we know with absolute shame that we have violated our relationships with others—with courage instead of alcohol. A drinking alcoholic who discovers his or her mistakes has a reflex response: "Give me a drink." A recovering alcoholic comes to the same moment and must then stop the old reflex and say, "I need forgiveness." That is the point of step ten, which also serves as introduction to the final two steps. We'll take step twelve first:

STEP TWELVE
Having had a spiritual experience as the result of these steps, we tried to carry this message to alcoholics, and to practice these principles in all our affairs.

The joy of living is the moving energy of those who say, "I am responsible. When anyone, anywhere, reaches out for help, I want the hand of AA always to be there. And for that, I am responsible."

Exciting, poignant, happy stories are told every day in thousands of AA meetings throughout North America. It is not my intention to write about twelfth-step work in my life. I only want to share with you the kinds of people who helped me and what rules of conduct they followed as they reached out to help.

The Christian people who helped me most were accepting, nonjudgmental, persistent, honest, open, loving, sincere, empathetic, intuitive, candid, quiet, and strong. Caring people can *cultivate* these qualities in their lives with the help of the Holy Spirit. And as they do, they will understand better the deeper meaning of this well-known proverb:

What we give away—we keep; for it is in the giving that we receive;
What we keep to ourselves—we lose; for in the keeping we cannot reproduce;
And when we die, we take with us only that which we have given away.

Because the Christian AA member knows that all other members are equally powerless over alcohol, he or she is quietly willing to let go, to let Christ do the healing work which is necessary. Living out of the strength which comes from the presence of the living Christ, the Christian recovering alcoholic willingly, gratefully, and unpretentiously carries a message of victory to other alcoholics. In the act of sharing the reality of Christ's healing, we continue to enjoy daily victory.

SEVEN
IN TOUCH
WITH GOD

Lead me in thy truth, and teach me, for thou art the God of my salvation; for thee I wait all the day long. Psalm 25:5, RSV

I began this story by letting you read what I wrote to the congregation where once I ministered. As I near the end of this simple story, I want to tell you the most important secret of my recovery. This secret is the warm, clear voice of my Savior which I hear in his Word. By means of daily meditation, I keep in touch with Christ. More accurately stated, in those times *he* keeps in touch with me.

The AA program focuses on keeping in touch with God in step eleven:

> STEP ELEVEN
> [We] sought through prayer and meditation to improve our conscious contact with God as we understood Him praying only for knowledge of His will for us and the power to carry that out.

Meditation with prayer is a personal adventure with God. Each one meditates and prayerfully maintains contact with God in a special and personal manner. One hardly knows where meditation ends and prayer begins. But there are at least four common traits that mark all true meditation and dynamic prayer.

First, there is *eager receptivity* for God's searching love. The Apostle John said, "We love because he first loved us." The Christian knows that God is the One who seeks the sinful, loves the lost, protects the powerless and nurtures the needy. All idol gods wait to be discovered by man, but God is the Discoverer, the Revealer, not the discovered.

In the Scriptures, we see from the opening chapters the pattern of God at work. All communication begins with him. When Adam and Eve slipped into sin, they did not cry out for God. On the contrary, they went into hiding and cowered even lower when they heard God coming with his questions: "Where are you? Have you eaten of the fruit? Who said that you were naked?" God sought out perplexed Noah and made a covenant with him. God laid his hand on Elijah, drafted him into prophetic service, and fed him, using ravens as delivery personnel. The Lord Jesus looked up at Zaccheus sitting in a tree, visited the lame man at a pool, stared across the room at Pilate, confronted Saul on the Damascus road. God's love is a seeking, electing, sovereign love. One waits receptively for God's searching love to find, nourish, and surprise one with his special gifts.

Second, there is *creative receptivity* as one waits for God to speak. Sometimes in meditation, one is creatively open, moving where God's words of invitation, promise, and instruction lead the heart. At other times one bears down with intense concentration, trying to channel thoughts while creatively listening to what God says. One tries to eliminate all interferences. Faith focuses on Christ in whom the believer is selected, redeemed, justified, sanctified, and glorified. With full concentration, the believer tries to embrace the broad realities of Christ's kingdom by focusing sharply on Christ the King.

Third, there is always *trusting receptivity,* an expectancy within the sinner's receptivity. Christ gives beyond what we could ask or think. He surprises us with peace, hope, and love beyond description. Because he knows the inner self more intimately than we know ourselves and because he cares in ways we never dreamed possible, we eagerly and expectantly wait for fresh miracles of Christ's providing love.

Fourth, gear your spirit into *patient receptivity.* In one of his parables, our Lord praised the persistent widow. He says that the one who perseveres to the end will gain the victory. More than a night watchman waits for morning, a meditating person waits for God's voice to speak. The poet puts it this way: "I waited patiently for the Lord; he inclined to me and heard my cry. He drew me up from the desolate pit, out of the miry bog, and set my feet upon a rock, making my steps secure. He put a new song in my mouth, a song of praise to our God" (Ps. 40:1-3, RSV).

GOD'S EFFECTIVE WORDS

The word "receptivity" forms the focus of life in meditation and prayer because the Christian centers all devotional activity in God's Word. Scriptural passages are not mere writings to be analyzed, words to be memorized, or ideas to be absorbed. They are not biblical mantras to be chanted for purposes of concentration. God's words of Scripture are alive, pregnant with powerful promise.

Among the resources at the close of this chapter is a listing of biblical texts grouped under the twelve steps of Alcoholics Anonymous. The texts provided there have no peculiar magic, but they have a profound message. Before sending anyone off to read texts, I want to underscore the Bible's unique power. It possesses amazing vitality and effectiveness. And this is true because the Person in the center of God's Word is himself "God's Word" (John 1:1)—Jesus Christ.

Jesus once said about his own words, "It is the Spirit that gives life, the flesh is of no avail; the words that I have spoken to you are spirit and life" (John 6:63, RSV). And the Christian knows by experience that Christ's words do become living water to satisfy the thirsty spirit; fire to warm the dark spirit of a frightened person; a chisel to break through the defenses of denial. His words are strong and effective for the listener.

The miracle which takes place in meditation can be stated a bit differently. The words about Jesus, his "gospel story" (good news), make the past event a present reality. What happened when he died on the cross is made alive, present, exciting, and real in the words of the Bible. His resurrection is given present power and reality in one's life in the words of the gospel when

97

those words are heard and obeyed. His acts of healing told in the miracle stories of the Bible take on contemporaneity, a "presentness," a today-it-happens-again quality. The words of the Bible are the vehicle which carries his personal voice to a person whom he calls by name.

When anyone reads, thinks about, and prays over the Lord's words recorded in the Bible, he or she may hear the indwelling Christ say, "I have spoken, and I will bring to pass what I have promised." So, when Jesus says, "Peace I leave with you, my peace I give unto you," his very words carry the treasure of his peace into one's life. Or when he says, "Your sins are forgiven," then his very words carry into one's life his forgiving love.

The Lord's words accomplish his purpose. Every time. Unquestionably. "For the word of God is living and active, sharper than any two-edged sword, piercing to the division of soul and spirit, of joints and marrow, and discerning the thoughts and intentions of the heart" (Heb. 4:12, RSV).

To the frightened alcoholic, seeking to hide from God and mankind and self, the gleaming two-edged sword may represent a terrifying threat. But to the Christian recovering alcoholic, the sword is nothing more than the Master's great scalpel, an instrument of miraculous healing, promising to all the possibility of victory over alcoholism.

THE TWELVE STEPS AND GOD'S WORD FOR MEDITATION AND PRAYER

STEP ONE
We admitted we were powerless over alcohol—that our lives had become unmanageable.

"My dwelling is plucked up and removed from me like a shepherd's tent; like a weaver I have rolled up my life; he cuts me off from the loom; from day to night thou dost bring me to an end; I cry for help until morning; like a lion he breaks all my bones; from day to night thou dost bring me to an end."

—Isaiah 38:12, 13, RSV

"Deep calls to deep at the thunder of thy cataracts; all thy waves and thy billows have gone over me."

—Psalm 42:7, RSV

"I am utterly spent and crushed; I groan because of the tumult of my heart."

—Psalm 38:8, RSV

"He [Jesus] was moved with compassion on them, because they fainted, and were scattered abroad, as sheep having no shepherd."

—Matthew 9:36, KJV

"I know that in me . . . dwelleth no good thing: for to will is present with me; but how to perform that which is good I find not."

—Romans 7:18, KJV

"The Lord is near to the brokenhearted, and saves the crushed in spirit."

—Psalm 34:18, RSV

"I am weary with my moaning; every night I flood my bed with tears; I drench my couch with my weeping. My eye wastes away because of grief, it grows weak because of all my foes. Depart from me, all you workers of evil; for the Lord has heard the sound of my weeping. The Lord has heard my supplication; the Lord accepts my prayer. All my enemies shall be ashamed and sorely troubled; they shall turn back, and be put to shame in a moment."

—Psalm 6:6-10, RSV

STEP TWO
[We] *came to believe that a power greater than ourselves could restore us to sanity.*

"He that dwelleth in the secret place of the most High shall abide under the shadow of the Almighty."

—Psalm 91:1, KJV

"My God shall supply all your need according to his riches in glory by Christ Jesus."

—Philippians 4:19, KJV

"I am persuaded, that neither death, nor life, nor angels, nor

principalities, nor powers, nor things present, nor things to come
. . . shall be able to separate us from the love of God which is in
Christ Jesus our Lord."

—Romans 8:38, 39, KJV

"O God, thou art my God, I seek thee, my soul thirsts for thee;
my flesh faints for thee, as in a dry and weary land where no
water is."

—Psalm 63:1, RSV

"O that I might have my request, and that God would grant my
desire. . . ."

—Job 6:8, RSV

"Cast away from you all the transgressions which you have
committed against me, and get yourselves a new heart and a new
spirit! . . . For I have no pleasure in the death of any one, says the
Lord God; so turn, and live."

—Ezekiel 18:31, RSV

"And Jesus answered them: 'Those who are well have no need
of a physician, but those who are sick; I have not come to call the
righteous, but sinners to repentance.' "

—Luke 5:31, RSV

"The eternal God is your dwelling place, and underneath are
the everlasting arms. And he thrust out the enemy before you,
and said, Destroy."

—Deuteronomy 33:27, RSV

"Casting all your care upon him; for he careth for you."

—1 Peter 5:7, KJV

STEP THREE
[We] *made a decision to turn our will and our lives over to the
care of God as we understand Him.*

"Ho, everyone that thirsteth, come ye to the waters, and he
that hath no money; come ye, buy, and eat. . . ."

—Isaiah 55:1, KJV

". . . He, being full of compassion, forgave their iniquity. . . .
For he remembered that they were but flesh; a wind that passeth
away, and cometh not again."

—Psalm 78:38, 39, KJV

"It is good that a man should both hope and quietly wait for the salvation of the Lord."

—Lamentations 3:26, KJV

"The name of the Lord is a strong tower; the righteous man runs into it and is safe."

—Proverbs 18:10, RSV

"But they who wait for the Lord shall renew their strength; they shall mount up with wings like eagles; they shall run, and not be weary; and they shall walk, and not faint."

—Isaiah 40:31, KJV

"Come to me, all who labor and are heavy laden, and I will give you rest. Take my yoke upon you, and learn from me; for I am gentle and lowly in heart, and you will find rest for your souls. For my yoke is easy, and my burden is light."

—Matthew 11:28-30, RSV

"Trust in the Lord with all your heart, and do not rely on your own insight. In all your ways acknowledge him, and he will make straight your paths."

—Proverbs 3:5, 6, RSV

"I waited patiently for the Lord; he inclined to me and heard my cry. He drew me up from the desolate pit, out of the miry bog, and set my feet upon a rock, making my steps secure."

—Psalm 40:1, 2, RSV

"Ask, and it will be given you; seek, and you will find; knock, and it will be opened to you."

—Matthew 7:7, RSV

STEP FOUR
[We] *made a searching and fearless moral inventory of ourselves.*

"He has showed you, O man, what is good; and what does the Lord require of you but to do justice, and to love kindness, and to walk humbly with your God?"

—Micah 6:8, RSV

"But if you have bitter jealousy and selfish ambition in your hearts, do not boast and be false to the truth. This wisdom is not such as comes down from above, but is earthly, unspiritual, devilish. For where jealousy and selfish ambition exist, there will be disorder and every vile practice."

—James 3:14-16, RSV

". . . Commune with your own heart upon your bed, and be still."

—Psalm 4:4, KJV

"For this very reason make every effort to supplement your faith with virtue, and virtue with knowledge, and knowledge with self-control, and self-control with steadfastness, and steadfastness with godliness, and godliness with brotherly affection, and brotherly affection with love."

—2 Peter 1:5-7, RSV

"Watch and pray that you may not enter into temptation; the spirit indeed is willing, but the flesh is weak."

—Matthew 26:41, RSV

"Do not boast about tomorrow, for you do not know what a day may bring forth."

—Proverbs 27:1, RSV

"Let not your hearts be troubled; believe in God, believe also in me."

—John 14:1, RSV

STEP FIVE
[We] *admitted to God, to ourselves, and to another human being the exact nature of our wrongs.*

"I said, I will confess my transgressions to the Lord."

—Psalm 32:5, RSV

"I prayed to the Lord my God and made confession. . . ."

—Daniel 9:4, RSV

"Cast your burden on the Lord, and he will sustain you; he will never permit the righteous to be moved."

—Psalm 55:22, RSV

"Therefore confess your sins to one another, and pray for one another, that you may be healed."

—James 5:16, RSV

"There are friends who pretend to be friends, but there is a friend who sticks closer than a brother."

—Proverbs 18:24, RSV

"Iron sharpens iron, and one man sharpens another."
—Proverbs 27:17, RSV

"The sacrifice acceptable to God is a broken spirit; a broken and contrite heart, O God, thou wilt not despise."
—Psalm 51:17, RSV

"In him we have redemption through his blood, the forgiveness of our trespasses, according to the riches of his grace which he lavished upon us."
—Ephesians 1:7, 8, RSV

"I have swept away your transgressions like a cloud, and your sins like mist; return to me, for I have redeemed you."
—Isaiah 44:22, RSV

"I am not aware of anything against myself, but I am not thereby acquitted. It is the Lord who judges me."
—1 Corinthians 4:4, RSV

STEP SIX
We're entirely ready to have God remove all these defects of character.

"I will sprinkle clean water upon you, and you shall be clean. . . ."
—Ezekiel 36:25, RSV

". . . How much more shall the blood of Christ, who through the eternal Spirit offered himself without spot to God, purge your conscience from dead works to serve the living God?"
—Hebrews 9:14, KJV

"If you sit down, you will not be afraid; when you lie down, your sleep will be sweet."
—Proverbs 3:24, RSV

"May the God of peace himself sanctify you wholly; and may your spirit and soul and body be kept sound and blameless at the coming of our Lord Jesus Christ. He who calls you is faithful, and he will do it."
—1 Thessalonians 5:23, 24, RSV

"And this is the confidence that we have in him, that, if we ask any thing according to his will, he heareth us."
—1 John 5:14, KJV

"If you abide in me, and my words abide in you, ask whatever you will, and it shall be done for you."

—John 15:7, RSV

STEP SEVEN
[We] *humbly asked Him to remove our shortcomings.*

"And whatever you ask in prayer, you will receive, if you have faith."

—Matthew 21:22, RSV

"Therefore I tell you, whatever you ask in prayer, believe that you have received it, and you will."

—Mark 11:24, RSV

"And if we know that he hears us in whatever we ask, we know that we have obtained the requests made of him."

—1 John 5:15, RSV

"No distrust made him waver concerning the promise of God, but he grew strong in his faith as he gave glory to God, fully convinced that God was able to do what he had promised."

—Romans 4:20, 21, RSV

"For I, the Lord your God, hold your right hand; it is I who say to you, 'Fear not, I will help you.' "

—Isaiah 41:13, RSV

"The angel of the Lord pitches camp around those who fear him; and he keeps them safe."

—Psalm 34:7, JB

"What then shall we say to this? If God is for us, who is against us? He who did not spare his own Son but gave him up for us all, will he not also give us all things with him?"

—Romans 8:31, 32, RSV

STEP EIGHT
[We] *made a list of all persons we had harmed, and became willing to make amends to them all.*

"You have heard that it was said to the men of old, 'You shall not kill; and whoever kills shall be liable to judgment.' But I say to you that every one that is angry with his brother shall be liable to

judgment; whoever insults his brother shall be liable to the council, and whoever says, 'You fool!' shall be liable to the hell of fire. So if you are offering your gift at the altar, and there remember that your brother has something against you, leave your gift there before the altar and go; first be reconciled to your brother, and then come and offer your gift."
—Matthew 5:21-24, RSV

"Argue your case with your neighbor himself, and do not disclose another's secret; lest he who hears you brings shame upon you, and your ill repute have no end."
—Proverbs 25:9, 10, RSV

". . . Return ye now every man from his evil way, and amend your doings. . . ."
—Jeremiah 35:15, KJV

". . . Behold, Lord, the half of my goods I give to the poor; and if I have defrauded any one of anything, I restore it fourfold."
—Luke 19:8, RSV

"Be strong and of good courage, do not fear or be in dread of them: for it is the Lord your God who goes with you; he will not fail you or forsake you."
—Deuteronomy 31:6, RSV

STEP NINE
[We] made direct amends to such people wherever possible, except when to do so would injure them or others.

"Bless those who persecute you; bless and do not curse them. Rejoice with those who rejoice, weep with those who weep. Live in harmony with one another; do not be haughty, but associate with the lowly; never be conceited. Repay no one evil for evil, but take thought for what is noble in the sight of all. If possible, so far as it depends upon you, live peaceably with all. Beloved, never avenge yourselves, but leave it to the wrath of God; for it is written, 'Vengeance is mine, I will repay, says the Lord.' No, 'if your enemy is hungry, feed him; if he is thirsty, give him drink; for by so doing you will heap burning coals upon his head.' Do not be overcome by evil, but overcome evil with good."
—Romans 12:14-21, RSV

"There are friends who pretend to be friends, but there is a friend who sticks closer than a brother."

—Proverbs 18:24, RSV

"Do not be deceived: 'Bad company ruins good morals.' "

—1 Corinthians 15:33, RSV

"He who walks with wise men becomes wise, but the companion of fools will suffer harm."

—Proverbs 13:20, RSV

"Do all things without grumbling or questioning, that you may be blameless and innocent, children of God without blemish in the midst of a crooked and perverse generation, among whom you shine as lights in the world. . . ."

—Philippians 2:14, 15, RSV

STEP TEN
[We] *continued to take personal inventory and when we were wrong we promptly admitted it.*

"Search me, O God, and know my heart! Try me and know my thoughts! And see if there be any wicked [hurtful] way in me, and lead me in the way everlasting!"

—Psalm 139:23, 24, RSV

"I am weary with my moaning; every night I flood my bed with tears; I drench my couch with my weeping. My eye wastes away because of grief, it grows weak because of all my foes. Depart from me, all you workers of evil; for the Lord has heard the sound of my weeping. The Lord has heard my supplication; the Lord accepts my prayer. All my enemies shall be ashamed and sorely troubled; they shall turn back, and be put to shame in a moment."

—Psalm 6:6-10, RSV

"Every way of man is right in his own eyes, but the Lord weighs the heart."

—Proverbs 21:2, RSV

"Cleanse thou me from secret faults."

—Psalm 19:12, KJV

"For by the grace given to me I bid every one among you not to think of himself more highly than he ought to think, but to think with sober judgment, each according to the measure of faith which God has assigned him."

—Romans 12:3, RSV

"Not that we are competent of ourselves to claim anything as coming from us: our sufficiency is from God. . . ."

—2 Corinthians 3:5, RSV

"Why do you see the speck that is in your brother's eye, but do not notice the log that is in your own eye?"

—Luke 6:41, RSV

STEP ELEVEN
[We] sought through prayer and meditation to improve our conscious contact with God as we understood Him, praying only for knowledge of His will for us and the power to carry it out.

"I bless the Lord who gives me counsel; in the night also my heart instructs me. I keep the Lord always before me; because he is at my right hand, I shall not be moved."

—Psalm 16:7, 8, RSV

". . . My eye grows dim with sorrow. Every day I call upon thee, O Lord; I spread out my hands to thee."

—Psalm 88:9, RSV

"He who gives heed to the word will prosper, and happy is he who trusts in the Lord."

—Proverbs 16:20, RSV

"Be still before the Lord, and wait patiently for him; fret not yourself over him who prospers in his way, over the man who carries out evil devices! . . . For the wicked shall be cut off; but those who wait for the Lord shall possess the land."

—Psalm 37:7, 9, RSV

"Thou dost keep him in perfect peace, whose mind is stayed on thee, because he trusts in thee. Trust in the Lord for ever, for the Lord God is an everlasting rock."

—Isaiah 26:3, 4, RSV

"Blessed is the man who walks not in the counsel of the wicked, nor stands in the way of sinners, nor sits in the seat of scoffers; but his delight is in the law of the Lord, and on his law he meditates day and night. He is like a tree planted by streams of water, that yields its fruit in its season, and its leaf does not wither. In all that he does, he prospers."

—Psalm 1:1-3, RSV

". . . Lead a life worthy of the Lord, fully pleasing to him, bearing fruit in every good work and increasing in the knowledge of God."

—Colossians 1:10, RSV

STEP TWELVE

[We] *having had a spiritual experience as the result of these steps, tried to carry this message to alcoholics and to practice these principles in all our affairs.*

". . . Go home to your friends, and tell them how much the Lord has done for you, and how he has had mercy on you."

—Mark 5:19, RSV

"He said also to the man who had invited him, 'When you give a dinner or a banquet, do not invite your friends or your brothers or your kinsmen or rich neighbors, lest they also invite you in return, and you be repaid. But when you give a feast, invite the poor, the maimed, the lame, the blind, and you will be blessed, because they cannot repay you. You will be repaid at the resurrection of the just."

—Luke 14:12-14, RSV

"For if they fall, one will lift up his fellow; but woe to him who is alone when he falls and has not another to lift him up."

—Ecclesiastes 4:10, RSV

"Through him then let us continually offer up a sacrifice of praise to God, that is, the fruit of lips that acknowledge his name. Do not neglect to do good and to share what you have, for such sacrifices are pleasing to God."

—Hebrews 13:15, 16, RSV

"Above all hold unfailing your love for one another, since love covers a multitude of sins."

—1 Peter 4:8, RSV

"And the King will answer them, 'Truly, I say to you, as you did it to one of the least of these my brethren, you did it to me.' "

—Matthew 25:40, RSV

EIGHT
THE ROAD AHEAD

The Lord will keep you from all evil; he will keep your life. Psalm 121:7, RSV

The soul searching involved in the writing of this book helped me bring order out of personal confusion. I will probably never know how and why alcoholism happened to me. But this I have learned: There is hope for the alcoholic. Christians who have experienced God's love in so many ways will wish to extend that love to any alcoholic who needs the special healing hand of God.

I will never forget the April day when I finally telephoned for help. My doctor was a young physician who at one time had been one of my theology students. Naturally, I was desperately afraid of the reaction of the religious community when they would learn that I had been hospitalized for alcoholism! To be treated for a malfunctioning gall bladder, heart, or even some emotional disorder would elicit sympathy. But to admit to being an alcoholic! This was not done openly. I had no idea what to expect.

My physician said this: "Alex, at school you helped me understand just what it means to trust the Lord more than I ever knew before. Why don't you try trusting him now?"

God used his words to shatter every defense I had so carefully built. No excuse remained. I had to submit to treatment and admit to my congregation that my problem was alcoholism. I needed their prayers.

God blessed this decision. He used many people, many prayers to help me along the path to recovery. Because of God's goodness to me I write this book to share whatever insights on alcoholism I am gaining so that others may walk with me on the road of sobriety. There is indeed help and hope for the alcoholic.

Let us suppose that there is an alcoholic in your family or that a friend's life is being damaged by alcohol. It's obvious to you that he has lost control over alcohol. Should you talk to him, warn him? His family has tried to do so, but these conversations usually ended in shouting matches followed by long periods of sullen silence on both sides. His wife is deeply concerned. He denies the existence of a problem. He says, "It's those pills I'm taking," or "It's those late nights spent in committee work that are taking their toll."

Denial, explained in chapter 3, must be penetrated if the alcoholic is to come to terms with his illness. But how must this be done? Must the alcoholic hit a skid-row "bottom" before he sees the light? Can friends and relatives do nothing more than pray?

Praise God, there is a method, a procedure, a technique, if you will, of confronting the alcoholic with his drinking patterns. It has proven successful in many cases. It is called "early intervention." Early intervention is a well-planned meeting between the alcoholic and carefully chosen persons whose concern for the welfare of the alcoholic motivates them. Their immediate goal is not to get him to stop drinking. That will not be accomplished immediately. Their goal is to get him to face the facts of his drinking. Early intervention is not the occasion to recite a litany of past misdeeds. This technique is never done in anger or for spite. It is an art learned by caring people to help problem drinkers break out of a world of illusion into the daily arena of reality.

Who must intervene? It is essential that those who intervene be carefully screened. They must possess enough emotional detachment to handle an angry exit, sullen inuendos, wounded denials. Often those who have suffered from the alcoholism of a family member cannot maintain this objectivity. Their wounds are too fresh and the pain too sharp. They will probably strike out at the person who brought so much grief into their lives. They will want to hurt him as they have been hurt. Therefore, persons who can remain objective must be chosen to intervene.

Secondly, to intervene you must have sorted out your own ideas about alcoholism. Earlier I discussed alcoholism as a sickness. Perhaps you do not hold this view and prefer to think of it in terms of sin. Whatever your viewpoint, be clear about it to yourself and open about it with the people you wish to help. Remember, the alcoholic can "feel" what you believe about alcohol, by your body language, attitudes, and voice tones, even more than by the words you speak. Educate yourself thoroughly on the subject before intervening. Bungled efforts by ill-prepared, well-intentioned people can do more harm than good.

Having chosen an intervention team, settle on a time and place when you will not be disturbed. The alcoholic must be sober. Because alcohol interferes with the brains's ability to reason, never try to sensibly discuss the problem when there has been some drinking.

While expressing their love and concern for the alcoholic, the team calmly presents facts. These must be carefully prepared. Present him with a description of alcohol-related events which have been witnessed. Include specific dates, amounts consumed, harmful effects. These facts should be written down so that when sensitive matters are brought up, such as religious values that have been unwittingly betrayed or innocent family members that have been deeply wounded, emotional control will be maintained. Use any evidence you can assemble. Photographs have been used. Handwriting comparisons have been laid before the alcoholic. Tape recordings of verbal abuse have been played. Use every bit of factual material you can gather in order to make the alcoholic realize how sick he really is.

I cannot emphasize too strongly that intervention must never be a list of accusations. It must be nonjudgmental. The alcoholic must never feel he is on trial. It is designed to be an eye-opener. Look! Here are the facts. You are sick! You need help. We love you and want you whole again. Please let us make you aware of your symptoms.

Remember, intervention is not designed to get the problem drinker to stop drinking. Much more is needed to achieve the fragile gift of sobriety. The intervention team should have previously decided on the treatment which they deem necessary for this alcoholic to maintain sobriety. You may at this point be able to elicit some well-intentioned promises from the alcoholic. He will "cut down." He will quit. Never again! You may consider the problem solved only to be disappointed in a month or two. Alcoholism is usually long in developing. A sincere promise will not make it go away. The alcoholic is powerless over the drug. Therefore he needs treatment. For this reason *solutions for the alcoholic are arranged before intervention takes place.* A proper treatment center should have been contacted, a bed reserved and transportation arranged. The alcoholic must have no time for a change of mind. Prompt, positive action is necessary. Do not fret about begrudging agreement, reluctant confessions, or sullen resentments. You cannot expect him to be happy about this turn of events. The team must be strong, loving, and decisive. The alcoholic's thanks will come later. It will come!

The alcoholic will react to what happens during the intervention session. If there has been no irrational explosion of anger or frozen, silent retreat into isolation, the problem drinker may himself offer a plan of corrective action. If honesty permits, compliment him on the choices suggested. Remember that his sense of self-esteem, already low because of growing guilt, has received another shattering blow. He has been given clear proof that he is not in control of his drinking. But allow him now the dignity of being involved in the decision-making process of what course of treatment to follow. Remember to treat the alcoholic as a human being. Depending on what plans he mentions, it will probably be necessary to take him a little farther along the road of healing and help. He will obviously choose the course which is least disruptive to his schedule, least painful to his psyche. Discuss plans A and B as they present themselves. Perhaps an alternate plan C can be suggested. If he is not informed about the function and purpose of AA meetings, be sure this information gets through to him. Tell family members of the help they can receive from Al-Anon and Alateen meetings. Interveners can often get the alcoholic to submit to the kind of treatment they as a team previously decided would be necessary.

What about treatment centers? Must Christian interveners

insist on Christian institutions? In the planning and educational phases of intervention, the team members should avail themselves of help from those people who possess Holy Spirit-nurtured sensitivities. Look for a treatment center where the spiritual dimensions of AA are wisely practiced. This needs emphasis. Healing horizons for many are limited narrowly to the boundaries of what one sees, feels, documents, and controls by experiment. So many professionals in health care are embarrassed to talk about God, prayer, Jesus Christ, confession, and salvation. The acids of cynicism and doubt have eaten gaping holes into the spiritual foundations of human need. I underscore strongly the need for religious and spiritual dynamics as we seek healing for the alcoholic.

A smorgasbord of self-help programs is available. Too often their methods ignore Christ and the deep religious needs of individuals. There are, despite the cynics, many alcoholics who are eager and able to talk about sin and guilt, righteousness and forgiveness, love and making amends, prayer and healing, hope and salvation, and many other religious realities.

Often in a problem drinker's life the spiritual dimensions are the first to stop functioning well. But even that "fact" is not always true. It wasn't in my case. It is true that it is impossible to discuss God and his grace intelligently with a person high or low on booze. But after the body has become drug free, the time may be just right to speak about such simple things as "Jesus loves me, this I know" and the realities of God and his judgment. For the Christian who is an alcoholic, these spiritual realities form the foundation for effective treatment.

In searching for a suitable treatment center do not be embarrassed about asking questions which arise out of your religious concerns. Staff members who will treat your loved one should be able to talk meaningfully using common theological terms. Ask them about the "Higher Power" in their program. What do they mean by "God as they understand him"? What is their idea of making amends, prayer and meditation, and many other concepts of the AA program? If they seem too embarrassed, ignorant, or sophisticated to talk about such things, you will know that this center is not the place of choice. I'm not saying that Christ cannot use such a treatment center. He can and does! But I would wish to choose a place where Christians work freely, openly, without apology, in the name of him who is the Savior and healer of life. Alcoholism untreated ends in death. The intervention team must be convinced that alcoholics will not—in fact, cannot—recover unless they learn to work steps two and three of AA's program with the help of those who know the Lord. Moreover, the problem drinker needs God in Christ to prepare himself for the kind of openness and honesty demanded to work steps four and five. Without the prayer and meditation spoken of in step eleven, the alcoholic will certainly relapse. Therefore, be sure to investigate the spiritual dimensions of the program offered by the treatment center you may choose.

One of the questions I am frequently asked concerns AA. How does the Christian fit into this group which has had such an impressive success record in helping alcoholics achieve and maintain the fragile gift of sobriety? Information about AA is plentiful and readily available. Read it carefully.

AA provides a simple and sound program that any alcoholic can follow. In a group of fellow alcoholics, one learns from the other to cultivate mutual understanding, acceptance, and help. There is only one condition to meet in order to become a part of this unique fellowship. There must be an honest desire to break away from drinking. Period. Beyond this there are no trial memberships, period pledges, or other commitments which are demanded.

AA is not a religious fellowship. No specific religious beliefs are set forth as a condition of membership. The Twelve Steps of the program may be interpreted by each member in his or her own way. AA's program is designed to help the problem drinker find an alcohol-free way of life. In meetings where I have been welcomed and found help, I remained free to tell my story. The twelve-step program can be used effectively by Christians as well as non-Christians. The alcoholic needs to be surrounded by others who understand and can empathize with his present problems and hopes for the future.

In my twelfth-step work of helping other alcoholics while I help myself, I'm often asked whether born-again believers ought to form their own groups. In answering both co-alcoholics who often attend Al-Anon meetings and alcoholics who attend closed meetings, I call attention to these facts: Attendance at meetings is fluid. One can move freely from one group to another. If one is not entirely comfortable with a certain group, he should try attending somewhere else. We urge each other to shop around for a meeting which fits. AA, Al-Anon, and Alateen are very democratic in structure, and, in theory, are committed to the spiritual dimensions of the AA program. I do not feel that special Christian groups are needed. More than once I've been helped as I listened to moving stories of Christ's healing power as a fellow alcoholic spoke about his or her Higher Power. I remember one instance in which a former agnostic told how he *came to believe* in Jesus Christ as his personal Savior. It is true, of course, there are AA meetings where specific Christian testimony is received with an embarrassed stare into a coffee cup or a dry cough. However, I have found that good experiences far outweigh the bad.

Some Christians are greatly disturbed by the profanity and objectionable language they heard at meetings. If this is dealt with in love and patience, it can usually be overcome. The sensitive alcoholic will usually avoid profanity and vulgarity if he realizes it is offensive to fellow members. But again, my advice is, search until a suitable meeting is found.

I urge people to openly seek out Christian treatment programs in hospitals, half-way houses, and other institutional settings. When it comes to weekly, daily meetings, I prefer to join my fellow pilgrims with drinking problems. Meetings are designed to preserve the delicate treasure of sobriety. They are not designed to win souls for Jesus or to engage in religious self-analysis.

In addition to AA meetings, there are meetings for those who do not have a personal drinking problem, but whose lives are as powerless over alcohol as is the sick person whom they love. These are Al-Anon and Alateen meetings.

Al-Anon was founded by families and relatives of alcoholics. It is a form of group interaction for the help of those who live with alcoholics. The people who live with the problem drinker learn that they are powerless to control the alcoholic's drinking, no matter how hard they try. The members of Al-Anon use the Twelve Steps of AA along with their own slogans. It is an anonymous fellowship. Everything shared in a meeting is held in strictest confidence.

This fellowship can build a person's confidence and serenity, equipping him to deal constructively and decisively with the alcoholic. The group fellowship enables the non-alcoholic parent to create a relatively normal environment for nurturing children. Empathetic participation in Al-Anon often leads to a reduction of anxiety, worry, and guilt. Many have been helped to find peace of mind, humility, and often a more dynamic development of their personal Christian commitment. As in AA, there is room for sharing in a Christian way the common and many-faceted problem of alcoholism.

Alateen is composed of young people from the ages of twelve through twenty who live in alcoholic family situations. There is group discussion, mutual encouragement, and learning of effective ways to cope with alcoholism as it affects teenagers' lives. In interaction with others, young people learn to exercise compassion rather than contempt for the alcoholic. Hopefully, they learn to develop some emotional detachment which helps the process of maturation. Together the members of Alateen try to build satisfying and rewarding life experiences for themselves.

Under the guidance of the indwelling Christ, hurting people find healing. These three groups, Alcoholics Anonymous, Al-Anon, and Alateen are joined by other alcoholic treatment centers as they work with the Twelve Step program devised by Bill and Bob in the early thirties. The spiritual dimensions of that simple model are congenial to a Christ-centered and a Scripture-matured way of life.

The *Big Book* is right when it states:

> Rarely have we seen a person fail who has thoroughly followed our path. Those who do not recover are people who cannot or will not completely give themselves to this simple program, usually men or women who are consti-tutionally incapable of being honest with themselves. . . . Remember that we deal with alcohol—cunning, baffling, powerful. Without help it is too much for us. But there is One who has all power—that one is God. May you find him now. . . .

116

Half measures availed us nothing. We stood at the turning point. We asked his protection and care with complete abandon.

Big Book, 3rd ed., pp. 58, 59

Meanwhile, every day the Lord says to me too:

"Lo, I am with you always to the close of the age."
[Matthew 28:20, RSV]

SELF-TEST
FOR DRINKERS

1. Do you enjoy a drink now and then?
2. Do you feel you are a normal drinker, that is, drink no more than the average?
3. Have you ever awakened the morning after some drinking the night before and found that you could not remember a part of the evening?
4. Do close relatives ever worry or complain about your drinking?
5. Can you stop drinking without a struggle after one or two drinks?
6. Do you ever feel guilty about your drinking?
7. Do friends or relatives think you are a normal drinker?
8. Are you always able to stop drinking when you want to?
9. Have you ever attended a meeting of Alcoholics Anonymous (AA) because of your drinking?
10. Have you gotten into physical fights when drinking?
11. Has drinking ever created problems between you and your wife, husband, parents, or near relatives?
12. Has your wife, husband, or other family member ever gone to anyone for help about your drinking?
13. Have you ever lost friendships because of your drinking?
14. Have you ever gotten into trouble at work because of drinking?
15. Have you ever lost a job because of drinking?

16. Have you ever neglected your obligations, your family or your work for two or more days in a row because you were drinking?
17. Do you ever drink in the morning?
18. Have you ever felt the need to cut down on your drinking?
19. Have there been times in your adult life when you have found it necessary to completely avoid alcohol?
20. Have you ever been told that you have liver trouble? Cirrhosis?
21. Have you ever had delirium tremens (DT's)?
22. Have you ever had severe shaking, heard voices, or seen things that weren't there after heavy drinking?
23. Have you ever gone to anyone for help about your drinking?
24. Have you ever been in a hospital because of drinking?
25. Have you ever been told by a doctor to stop drinking?
26. Have you ever been a patient in a psychiatric hospital or on a psychiatric ward in a general hospital?
27. Was drinking part of the problem that resulted in that hospitalization?
28. Have you ever been a patient at a psychiatric or mental health clinic or gone to any doctor, social worker, or clergyman for help with any emotional problems?
29. Have you ever been arrested, even for a few hours, because of drunken behavior (not driving)?
30. Have you ever been arrested, even for a few hours, because of driving while intoxicated? How many times?
31. Have your parents ever had problems with alcohol?
32. Have your brothers or sisters ever had problems with alcohol?
33. Has your husband (or wife) ever had problems with alcohol?
34. Have any of your children ever had problems with alcohol?

The typical alcoholic's response to questions 2, 5, 7, and 8 would be no. The typical alcoholic's response to all other questions would be yes.

Anyone who scores 10 or more typical alcoholic's responses in this self-administered test is very likely to be alcoholic. A score of 7-9 typical alcoholic's responses would indicate a strong possibility of alcoholism.

SELF-TEST FOR
FAMILY MEMBERS

1. Do you lose sleep because of a problem drinker?
2. Do most of your thoughts revolve around the problem drinker or problems that arise because of him or her?
3. Do you exact promises about the drinking which are not kept?
4. Do you make threats to a drinker in the family and not follow through on them?
5. Has your attitude fluctuated toward this problem drinker (alternating between love and hate)?
6. Do you mark, hide, dilute, and/or empty bottles of liquor or medication?
7. Do you think that everything would be OK if only the problem drinker would stop or control the drinking?
8. Do you feel alone, fearful, anxious, angry, or frustrated most of the time? Are you beginning to feel dislike for yourself and to wonder about your sanity?
9. Do you find *your* moods fluctuating widely—as a direct result of the problem drinker's moods and actions?
10. Do you feel responsible and guilty about the drinking problem?
11. Do you try to conceal, deny, or protect the problem drinker?
12. Have you withdrawn from outside activities and friends because of embarrassment and shame over the drinking problem?

13. Have you taken over many chores and duties that you would normally expect the problem drinker to assume?
14. Do you feel forced to try to exert tight control over the family expenses with less and less success? And are financial problems increasing?
15. Do you feel the need to justify your actions and attitudes and, at the same time, feel somewhat smug and self-righteous when you compare yourself to the drinker?
16. If there are children in the house, do they often take sides with either the problem drinker or the spouse?
17. Are the children showing signs of emotional stress, such as withdrawal, having trouble with authority figures, or rebelling?
18. Have you noticed physical symptoms in yourself, such as nausea, a knot in the stomach, ulcers, shakiness, sweating palms, or bitten fingernails?
19. Do you feel utterly defeated that nothing you can say or do will move the problem drinker? Do you believe he or she can't get better?
20. Where this applies, is your sexual relationship with a problem drinker affected by feelings of revulsion? Do you "use" sex to manipulate, or refuse sex to punish him or her?

A yes to any five of these questions probably indicates that alcoholism exists in the family and is producing negative changes in the person answering them.

RESOURCES

ACES (ADDICTION CONSULTATION
        AND EDUCATIONAL SERVICES)
126 North Des Plaines
Chicago, Illinois 60606
(312) 236-5172 ext. 335

AL-ANON FAMILY GROUPS HEADQUARTERS, INC.
P. O. Box 812, Madison Square Station
New York, New York 10010
(212) 475-6110

ALCOHOL AND DRUG PROBLEMS OF NORTH AMERICA
1130 Seventeenth Street, NW
Washington, D.C. 20036

ALCOHOLICS ANONYMOUS
P. O. Box 459
Grand Central Station
New York, New York 10017

HAZELDEN LITERATURE DEPARTMENT
Box 176
Center City, Minnesota 55012
(800) 328-9288 toll free

NATIONAL CLEARINGHOUSE
    FOR ALCOHOL INFORMATION
P. O. Box 2345
Rockville, Maryland 20852
(301) 948-4450

NATIONAL COUNCIL ON ALCOHOLISM, INC.
2 Park Avenue
New York, New York 10016

In all fifty states the Department of Mental Health and
Development Disabilities (or related title names) has a department dealing with alcoholism and drug abuse. Your telephone
directory provides appropriate addresses and phone numbers.
The Canadian Government provides similar health services.

The Yellow Pages, under such words as "Alcoholism Information
and Treatment Centers," is a helpful point of local contact to find
out more about this insidious disease and helpful resources.